PAUL

WITH MICHAEL ASHLEY

THE
DISSOLUTION
SOLUTION

A Divorce Lawyer's Advice on
the Best Ways to Part Ways

RIVER GROVE
BOOKS

Published by River Grove Books
Austin, TX
www.rivergrovebooks.com

Distributed by River Grove Books

Design and composition by Greenleaf Book Group
Cover design by Greenleaf Book Group
Cover images used under license from ©Shutterstock.com/Saynisa

Publisher's Cataloging-in-Publication data is available.

Paperback ISBN: 978-1-63299-739-5

eBook ISBN: 978-1-63299-740-1

Hardcover ISBN: 978-1-63299-748-7

First Edition

CONTENTS

FOREWORD

Paul Nelson is a locally well-known divorce lawyer who makes it quite clear that he has experience in the area he writes about, having gone through a divorce himself.

"I've personally experienced all the pain, the anger, the rage, the self-loathing, the doubts, the recriminations, the resentments, the second-guessing, the sleepless nights, and the blessed relief that's part and parcel of the divorce experience," he writes in his introduction.

I might be one of the least qualified people to write a foreword for this book, since I've been married to my wife for thirty-one years. What I do know are thousands of business owners and entrepreneurs who have built their company from the ground up, treating it like their baby, and don't want the business to fall apart because of a serious personal matter like a divorce.

Paul writes expertly about the spouse who in 2005 sought $18 million from her husband, a real estate developer who offered $11 million. It was bad timing, because the 2008 financial crisis damaged his business, and she got $5 million instead in 2015, after negotiations dragged on for years.

In another case, a divorce that started amicable ended in bitterness when the wife found out that her husband had spent $10,000 on a necklace for his mistress and he found out she had forged documents allowing her to siphon money from their company. "Eventually, all hell broke loose, the fangs came out, and what was supposed to be a quick, simple, and *inexpensive* divorce dragged on for three years," Paul explains. "The moral? You can *intend* to have a quick and simple low-cost divorce, but it's a crapshoot. And as in craps, the odds are *never* in your favor."

This book gives plenty of advice that I've wondered about over the years. For example, does a prenuptial agreement foreshadow gloom and doom for what should be a happy wedding? Paul argues no.

Prenups "help thwart divorce because the act of completing one forces a couple to contemplate worst-case scenarios *before* committing to a union," Paul writes. "It lowers the veil of romance and makes people look at nuptials using cold, hard reality. It also allows couples to know in advance what they will take—and not take—from a marriage upon its dissolution. If the spouses know they won't be able to take each other to the cleaners, they're more likely to look for ways to resolve their differences." That advice is extremely good for anyone with any assets.

The book is chock-full of stories, some of which are quite funny or dramatic and could be scenes from *L.A. Law*. Take the ex-wife who claimed she couldn't work because of physical problems but ably showed the judge her six-inch Jimmy Choo shoes. She lost her argument. Paul also tells of having drinks with a client who, at the end of the case, acknowledged that he was blinded by spite and that he could have saved himself and his bank account by working harder to protect his investment of more than twenty years. "I picked up the tab for the drinks. After all, he was already out $137,000," Paul quips.

Foreword

The book has interesting tidbits, such as that the price of an average divorce in California is $17,000 without children and $26,500 with children. The most expensive divorce in history occurred in 2019, when Jeff Bezos paid his then-wife with stock in Amazon, which at that time was worth $38 billion, or ten times the value of the second-most-expensive divorce.

I love Paul's list of ten top reasons to stay married: three of them are "the kids." He tells the story of a bitter custody battle that devasted a couple's two teenage daughters—one posted naked pictures of herself on Instagram, and the other dropped out of high school and used drugs.

Paul gives this perceptive analysis: "Mental health experts will tell you a divorce, even a so-called amicable one, can leave deep, lasting scars on the psyches of everyone involved, especially children. While a marriage can be dissolved, the pain a parental breakup creates can often last a lifetime."

It's odd that a lawyer would want to discourage potential clients from getting a divorce that would economically benefit him, which demonstrates his desire to help people. He says that there's a 40 to 50 percent chance a marriage will end prematurely—and that's just for the first marriage. The divorce rate for second marriages increases to over 60 percent.[1]

Paul writes expertly on how to pick a lawyer and what to expect at a trial. He notes that no one wants to be considered a loser in a divorce case; on the other hand, each person must ask: What does winning look like?

Paul rounds out the book with plenty of witty aphorisms, such as "No one gets divorced because they feel good about how things are going." It's also humorous to see a lawyer exhibit self-deprecation.

When Paul writes about the reasons to get married, he includes this line: "Oh, have I left out the romantic part? Must be the lawyer in me."

Peter J. Brennan
Executive editor of the *Orange County Business Journal*

INTRODUCTION

I t had been a perfect wedding. Rachel had picked the venue, a hundred-year-old winery in California's Santa Inez Valley. Jeff had hired the band, a six-member ensemble that could play everything from 1940s Broadway show tunes to the latest mumble rap. After dating for more than three years and having watched many of their friends wed—then divorce—the two were determined to make their marriage last.

They *would* work out their problems. They *would* learn to compromise. Love, they believed, would indeed conquer all. Yet, five years and two children later, here they were, standing before a judge preparing to sign papers of marital dissolution.

How could it all go so wrong?

Divorce has been likened to death. It's sad. It's tragic.

It's also a fact of life.

Although specific numbers vary, experts will tell you there's a 40 to 50 percent chance a marriage will end prematurely.[1] The odds of dissolution depend on many factors, like the age at which the spouses wed,[2] household earnings (as income drops, divorce rates rise),[3] a history of prior divorce (yes, divorce can become a habit!),[4] where the couple lives (in 2023, Nevada has the highest split rate, Massachusetts the lowest),[5] and even whether the couple lived together before tying the knot ("shacking up" increases the odds of breakup).[6]

Almost no one goes into a marriage expecting to get divorced. But if it happens, it's best to be prepared. And that's what this book is about. Now, they say you should never trust a skinny chef or a fat doctor. By this measure, you also shouldn't trust a family law attorney who hasn't been divorced.

Guess what. I've been there. I've done the deed. I've personally experienced all the pain, the anger, the rage, the self-loathing, the doubts, the recriminations, the resentments, the second-guessing, the sleepless nights, and the blessed relief that's part and parcel of the divorce experience.

As a practicing family law attorney for a quarter century, I have also shepherded hundreds of clients through this same difficult experience. I have seen the anxiety, the confusion, and the depression my clients endure when "to love, honor, and cherish" devolves into passionless property settlements and contentious child visitation schedules.

As an empathetic person, I wish to minimize that suffering as much as possible. I figure if people know what to expect, they'll be better able to deal with the trauma divorce inflicts. That's why I wrote this book.

My beat is Southern California, specifically Orange County. More specifically, fabled Newport Beach, ground zero for Fox's early 2000s hit show *The O.C.* If you're going to practice divorce law, this is the place to do it.

The reasons people here in Orange County divorce are little different than they are elsewhere in the Western world: money problems (yes, even the rich have financial difficulties), infidelity, domestic violence, and boredom.

Introduction

I also suspect a key reason the divorce rate here runs so high is frustration with unfulfilled expectations. People in SoCal dream big and desire perfection. It's baked into the culture. And when people's aspirations don't come to fruition, when even wealth and success fail to deliver personal happiness and satisfaction, they fight, blame the other, and look for an escape hatch.

And that's where people like me come in.

Being a family law attorney makes me part legal counselor, part therapist, part father confessor, part life coach, part money manager, and part mediator. It also makes me a hired gun. A 50-caliber Gatling gun. An unstoppable war machine.

As for my track record, my clients will tell you I do a damn good job. Because I understand the law. Because I'm tough. And because I know how to tell a compelling story. There's an old saying in the legal business: "The person with the best story wins," and I take that as gospel.

A study of legal giants like Richard Posner, Cass Sunstein, Ronald Dworkin, and Oliver Wendell Holmes is incomplete without a similar appreciation for storytellers like Charles Dickens, Stephen King, and Walt Disney. I can tell you from experience that even the most hardened judge—let alone an impressionable jury—can be swayed by a compelling narrative.

My affinity for stories explains why this book is packed with them. I believe there is no better way to make a point than to present a case study. Here I must emphasize that because professional ethics forbids me from sharing my clients' personal particulars, all the tales I offer have been fictionalized to protect privacy. In other words, while the problems, strategies, and outcomes I present within these pages are all very real, names, descriptions, and dialogue are imaginary. (As much as I want to offer you a compelling read, I also want to keep my law license.)

Also, although this book is traditionally structured, don't feel obligated to read it in linear sequence. Look at it as a how-to book of tips and tricks to absorb in whatever order suits your needs and fancy. I hope you find it engaging, informative, and perhaps even fun (as much as a book about divorce can be a good time). And when you're done, keep it as a handy reference. The thing about divorce—especially when children are involved—is that while it may be final, it's never quite over.

1

DIVORCE HAPPENS

A good marriage is one where each partner secretly
believes they got the better deal.

—Anonymous

Why do people get married?

The answer depends on where and when you're talking about. Anthropologists tell us for most of human history, the traditional lifelong union of one man and one woman did not exist.[1] For tens of thousands of years, the sexes lived as nomadic hunter-gatherers in groups of thirty or fewer. Back then, the male "chief" generally had first pick of all available females, the lesser males pairing up with whatever females happened to be free for a casual dalliance. "Trading women" between passing tribes helped to promote genetic diversity and avoid inbreeding dangers.

It wasn't until agriculture's invention and the idea of "private property" that codified marriage was invented—mostly to establish legitimate inheritance. (This occurred in the Middle East about four thousand years ago.) By legally binding a woman to a man, it was easier to determine a man's legitimate heirs.

So much for romance and Valentine's Day. In other words, marriage was about *property transfer*. Still, many unions weren't monogamous. Kings not only had many wives but often had dozens of concubines for sexual variety. Even lowly shepherds, like Old Testament patriarchs, had more than one spouse. (What happened to all the excess males? They tended to die in battle.) Among the nobility, marriage was used to forge political alliances, preserve family fortunes, and yes, end wars. Even among the lower classes, women were viewed as little more than chattel and marriage a mercantile activity.

With Christianity came the idea of marriage as a "holy sacrament" the Church could legitimize.[2] (This occurred in the fifth century AD.) Only then, in the late Middle Ages, came the radical concept of romantic love. For the first time, men and women entertained the notion they could pair up with someone for whom they shared a mutual attraction, maybe even affection. And yet marriages to extend family lines, acquire titles and/or property, or expand social or political influence persisted. In many cultures, parents continued to arrange marriages with the heads of other local families or via matchmakers. (This tradition still exists in South Asian cultures and within religiously conservative communities like Ultra-Orthodox Jews.)[3]

You could argue it wasn't until the early twentieth century that true *modern marriage*, one based on mutual love, shared respect, and joint responsibility, became the norm. Many factors contributed to this turn of events:

- Women in the United States and Europe got the vote, becoming equal citizens.

- The rise of mass media, influencing heart and minds.

- The invention of "the pill," allowing women to become sexually independent.

Also, with the Supreme Court rulings of the early twenty-first century legalizing same-sex marriages, the idea that a marriage could only be between one man and one woman has also gone by the wayside. Yet, even as Western culture venerates the idea of love-based marriage, other reasons explain why people decide to permanently come together. These include the following.

Companionship. Some people are literally "married to their best friend." They enjoy each other's company but lack the passion or sexual spark we associate with marital bliss. In these arrangements, the spouses may enjoy casual sexual encounters or even long-term relationships with others but in the end, still return to each other.

Kids. When a casual sexual encounter produces a pregnancy, the couple may decide to wed for the sake of the children. They tie the knot not out of love, but from a sense of duty.

Ego/status. We all know the stereotype: The rich, successful, middle-aged man who ditches his old spouse for a newer model—the so-called trophy wife. It may be a stereotype, but it's rooted in truth. In fact, here in Newport Beach, it's not so much a stereotype as a cliché.

Legal/financial advantages. The law provides advantages to married couples, and some people decide to get hitched just to leverage these benefits. The extreme case is the so-called Green Card Marriage, in which a noncitizen weds an American citizen to stay and work legally in the United States.

Whatever *your* reason for marrying, I sincerely hope your union is a long and happy one. Of course, if it *is*, then you're probably not reading this book.

FROM *GUINNESS WORLD RECORDS, 2022*

Longest marriage: Herbert and Zelmyra Fisher were married eighty-six years, nine months, and sixteen days as of February 27, 2011. Sadly, that's also when Herbert passed away at 106 years old.

Most married woman in the world: Linda Wolfe of Anderson, Indiana. She was married a whopping twenty-three times, her first at age sixteen.

Most marriage vow renewals: Lauren and David Blair from Hendersonville, Tennessee, who wed in 1980, formally exchanged vows a hundred times prior to Linda's passing in 2010 at age sixty-nine.

Most expensive nuptials: The record goes to Sheikh Mohammed bin Zayed bin Sultan Al Nahyan, crown prince of Abu Dhabi and Princess Salama. Their extravagant 1981 wedding clocked in at $100 million. (That's more than $317 million in 2022 dollars.)

Do You Really Want a Divorce?

We've discussed why people wed. Now we must ask: Why do people get divorced? Nineteenth-century Russian novelist Leo Tolstoy famously wrote, "All happy families resemble one another; every unhappy family is unhappy in its own way."[4] However, this is not true when it comes to divorce. For the most part, the reasons couples split tend to be quite standard. These include:

- Money problems

- Extramarital affairs

- Conflict over family responsibilities

- Substance abuse/alcoholism

- Physical/emotional abuse

- Lack of emotional/physical intimacy

- Lack of commitment/restlessness

- Diverging interests and ambitions

We've all heard that opposites attract. To a large extent, this is true. There's something exciting about the foreign and exotic. Differences have been the basis for initial attraction and infatuation since the dawn of time. Like the yin and yang, stark differences can complement the other.

But it's when differences become the *basis for marriage* that trouble often starts. Over time those qualities that once attracted you to your partner can repel you. What most people want are others who *mirror* themselves. Partners who aren't *exact* duplicates, yet similar enough in most ways as to be recognizable. People who share an affinity for the same foods. The same sports. (Or who don't like sports at all.) Who watch the same kinds of movies and TV shows. Who enjoy the same recreational activities. Who share a similar sense of humor.

Likewise, if the differences between partners are fundamental, resentment can build, creating pressure until finally it all explodes. Examples include the following:

- You want to live in the city, and your partner likes the country.

- You dig parties, and your partner likes to stay home and read.

- You like to spend money freely, and your partner watches every penny.

- You desire children, and your partner does not.

These kinds of differences can breed resentment. Over time, bitterness can set in, morphing into anger, even hatred. There may come a point when neither of you wants to look at the other, much less share the same bed.

That's when divorce happens.

But wait. Are you sure? Are you really, *really* sure? Because when you commit to a divorce, you're stepping onto the express elevator to hell. I'm talking about a world of pain.

First, there will be financial pain. Yes, filing for a divorce only costs a few hundred dollars, but any couple with assets—a home, vehicles, investments—will need legal representation. And divorce lawyers aren't cheap. Also, the more assets you have, the more expensive they become. In California, where the cost of divorce is 35 percent higher than the national average, the price of a simple, uncontested divorce currently averages $17,000 for couples without children, and $26,500 for couples *with* children.[5]

If the divorce is contested, the price tag can balloon into the hundreds of thousands of dollars. And that's if you're lucky. As I like to say, if you want to be a multimillionaire, stay married.

The Case of the Disheartened Optimists

It's time for our first interlude. This is the tale of Jake and Jane. Jake was a successful business owner. Jane was an equally successful medical professional. Married in their early thirties, their paths diverged as career demands kept them separated for increasingly extended periods. After fifteen years of marriage, during which they produced one child, a girl, now ten, they realized they had no more passion for one another.

They agreed that a divorce was in both their best interests.

One thing Jake and Jane wanted to avoid was a long, costly court fight. "The only people who make money in a divorce are the lawyers," Jake liked to say. But, as with many non-W-2 professionals, the couple's finances were complicated, and *someone* had to determine who was owed what. Then there was custody to work out.

Jane suggested they go the mediation route. Jake agreed.

Mediation is a process whereby a neutral arbiter, the *mediator*, collaborates with both parties to work out an equitable, legally binding settlement. As with a judge, the mediator's decision is final and not subject to appeal. The purported advantage is that mediation is private and can be relatively quick and inexpensive.

The operative words here are "can be." In fact, Jake and Jane struggled through weeks of back and forth with their mediator, each offer triggering a counteroffer with little progress being made.

Then the dirt came out.

To her horror, Jane learned Jake once spent $10K on a necklace for a woman he was cheating with. Meanwhile, Jake discovered Jane had forged documents allowing her to siphon money from their company. Eventually, all hell broke loose, the fangs came out, and what was supposed to be a quick, simple, and *inexpensive* divorce dragged on for three years. Worse, it cost Jake and Jane hundreds of thousands in legal fees.

The moral? You can *intend* to have a quick and simple low-cost divorce, but it's a crapshoot. And as in craps, the odds are *never* in your favor.

The poverty rate of divorced women is 27 percent, nearly three times the rate for divorced men.[6]

Other Costs Abound

Beyond hefty legal bills, be prepared for emotional suffering. Not just the pain of watching your hopes and dreams smashed to smithereens, but the agony of being forced to relive the worst parts of your relationship like Malcolm McDowell in *A Clockwork Orange*—strapped to a chair with your eyes pinned open.

Okay. Not a pretty sight, I know. But this is especially true if your divorce is contested, and each party is compelled to paint the other in the worst possible light. By the time the lawyers are done, you'll truly hate your ex—and yourself. Ask: Is that what you really want to sign up for?

So, before you head down this path, also ask yourself, "Have I exhausted all other possible options?" Because, all things considered, divorce should truly be treated as a last resort.

Divorce is one of the *biggest* reasons people fail to accumulate wealth.[7]

The Case of the Malicious Marketers

A few years back, a litigation attorney and accountant, both of whom I respected greatly, asked me to represent a woman who had *already* been in process of divorce for nearly half a decade.

Normally, I won't be "the third attorney." Yes, I understand a person wanting new legal representation. *Once*. But if someone keeps cycling through lawyers like they change underwear, that's a blazing red flag.

Worse, this woman had already hired—and fired—five or six prior attorneys. Which is not a red flag. It's a screaming, fifty-foot-tall, Run for Your Life electric billboard you can see from low orbit.

Still, I decided to accept the case based on my professional relationship with these individuals. The woman and her husband (we'll call them Betty and Bill) owned one of the largest marketing firms in OC. Bill ran the video/content/media division while Betty handled client management. (Think: *Mad Men*.) They had literally hundreds of employees working out of nine offices throughout SoCal. I estimated their business valuation between $35 million and $45 million at the time divorce papers were filed.

The major point of contention between Bill and Betty was not one of fidelity, abuse, or even "irreconcilable differences," but *fiduciary responsibility*. Their company was in dire financial straits, and each blamed the other for their troubles, both before and during their separation. At stake? The division of $10 million held in an attorney-client trust account and the debt assignment from the business's demise.

I represented Betty in the dispute for a year, during which each party spent more than $500,000 in attorney and forensic fees. (And this was on top of the hundreds of thousands of dollars they'd burned in the previous half-decade before I joined the case.)

Ultimately, we went to trial with a private judge. Proceedings lasted three weeks. During this time, opposing counsel regularly made settlement offers to limit the damage of the judge's decision, one that was, by definition, uncertain. At one point, Bill even offered what was the equivalent of $4 million in cash and real estate just to end this nightmare.

My own forensic accountant and I prepared three different likely scenarios to illustrate why this was, from Betty's standpoint, an excellent offer. We advised her that if the judge ruled she (and she alone) had indeed breached her fiduciary responsibility, she could end up with literally nothing.

But Betty insisted she was blameless in this affair and so refused anything her estranged husband proposed. She stood on principle—and it cost her. At the end of the three-week-long ordeal, the worst-case scenario came true. The judge ruled completely against her and in favor of Bill, costing her a total of $10 million when viewed against the best offer we earlier proposed.

The moral of the story: In divorces, emotions run high. (No one gets divorced because they feel good about how things are going.) Yet stubbornness can lead to bad outcomes. And trials always come with a high element of risk.

A divorce is much like a home remodeling project. Estimate the time and cost involved—then multiply it by two.

TOP TEN REASONS TO STAY MARRIED

1. Married folks live longer than single people.

2. Tax breaks.

3. The kids.

4. You get higher Social Security payments.

5. There's someone to scratch your back.

6. The kids.

7. Inheritance implications.

8. Health insurance benefits.

9. Decreased chance of clinical depression.

10. The kids.

Remember Why You Got Married in the First Place

I am not a therapist. I have no formal mental health training. I've never even *been* in therapy. But I have gleaned some wisdom through my years as a divorce lawyer. Feel free to skip this section if you have a good therapist. Take their advice, not mine.

That said, if you're conflicted over the idea of divorce—and you probably should be—it helps to consider why you got married in the first place.

As discussed, there are many reasons why people marry, and your marriage likely encompasses many of them. Marriage provides couples with stability and a handy sexual partner—*no more dating!*—as well as a secure environment to raise children. Marriage also provides adults with a sense of legitimacy—it's the *thing grown-ups do*—as well as a raft of nifty financial and tax benefits. And marriage helps ensure money and property get passed along to those whom you have already passed along your DNA.

Oh, have I left out the romantic part? Must be the lawyer in me.

Qualities that traditionally draw couples together include sexual attraction, mutual interests, senses of humor, shared religious convictions (or lack thereof), shared worldviews (including political affiliations), and similar values, beliefs, and life goals. The relationship is then strengthened by qualities like honesty, fidelity, intimacy, communication, and respect.

If your estranged spouse possessed these qualities when you decided to marry, chances are they're still there. Your challenge is to rediscover what made you fall in love in the first place and hopefully save both of you emotional and financial grief that may damage you for life.

Think of the Children

Estranged couples are encouraged to stay together "for the sake of the children." It's a cliché, but there's a more than a kernel's worth of wisdom in it.

Divorce can devastate young ones. Kids have an innate need for structure, routine, and certainty. Although the effects of divorce vary from child to child and can be influenced by age, studies show divorce produces a variety of negative impacts on a young person's psyche, behavior, and even ability to develop healthy long-term relationships.[8]

Common problems associated with parental divorce include:

- Feelings of guilt

- Lowered academic achievement

- Anger/irritability

- Health problems

- Difficulties adapting to change

- Antisocial behavior/violence

Although there are often good reasons for getting a divorce, such as spousal abuse when children are involved, couples should make every effort to work through their problems and seek amicable accommodation.

The Case of the Peevish Parents

Todd and Jennifer had just celebrated their twentieth wedding anniversary when they decided to part ways. When it came to the property side of the divorce, the dissolution looked simple. Both were W-2 employees. They owned no real estate beyond their three-bedroom house in Corona del Mar. Their liquid assets, including a modest stock portfolio, topped out at less than $100,000.

A simple fifty-fifty split was agreeable to both.

What Todd and Jennifer could not agree on was primary child custody. They had two teen daughters, and each accused the other of being an unfit parent. Todd blamed Jennifer of being an alcoholic. Jennifer called Todd an absent father. Each claimed to be a pillar of virtue and accused the other of compulsive lying.

While Todd and Jennifer thought they were doing right by their daughters in fighting for custody, their unrelenting hostility had a bad effect on both girls. The youngest, fifteen years old, "acted out" by posting naked photos of herself on Instagram and dating men five years her senior. The eldest, seventeen, got deep into drugs and dropped out of high school midway through her junior year.

Mental health experts will tell you a divorce, even a so-called amicable one, can leave deep, lasting scars on the psyches of everyone involved, especially children.[9] While a marriage can be dissolved, the pain a parental breakup creates can often last a lifetime.

What Are the Alternatives?

If you want to save your marriage, you have options to consider. Depending on your circumstances, they may be tried individually or in combination. These include:

- Couples counseling (with a licensed therapist)

- Spiritual counseling (with a priest/pastor/rabbi/imam)

- Financial counseling (with a certified financial advisor)

- Reading printed guides to marriage and divorce (like this one)

- Have more sex (it works!)

The Tale of the $137,000 Martini

One of my Southern California clients completed a divorce that cost him a cool $137,000. A few weeks after the divorce finalized, we met for a drink at the bar of a posh Laguna Beach hotel. Over martinis, we reviewed his case and discussed all the things he *could* have done, had he been so inclined, to save his marriage. He finally admitted that, yes, he had been blinded by spite and could have saved himself—and his bank account—pain by working harder to protect his "investment" of more than twenty years.

I picked up the tab for the drinks. After all, he was already out $137,000.

Prenups Save Marriages?

One way to avert divorce in the first place is to create a prenuptial agreement, a so-called prenup, before ever walking down the aisle. Key story elements in classic movies like *Liar, Liar* (1997) and *Body Heat* (1981), a prenup is a contract signed by both parties before marrying. It details how finances will be handled during marriage and divided between spouses should they break up.

Imagine a couple, Ted and Mary. Prior to matrimony, Mary owned a condominium townhouse. Ted rented an apartment. After deciding they would move into Mary's place upon marrying, they stated in the prenup the property would remain in her name and any payments made to reduce the principal loan would remain her separate property.

In the event of divorce, the townhouse is 100 percent Mary's. Absent the prenup, Ted would likely gain a financial interest in the townhouse because principal payments are made from community funds. Depending on the marriage length, this could be a large sum. Not to mention the costs to prove that issue at trial.

But prenups are relevant to our discussion for another reason. They help thwart divorce because the act of completing one forces a couple to contemplate worst-case scenarios *before* committing to a union. It lowers the veil of romance and makes people look at nuptials using cold, hard reality. It also allows couples to know in advance what they will take—and not take—from a marriage upon its dissolution. If the spouses know they won't be able to take each other to the cleaners, they're more likely to look for ways to resolve their differences.

The Case of the Starry-Eyed Bride

Since Heather was a child, she fantasized about her dream wedding. She had picked out the flowers: *Ranunculus*. She had chosen the wedding cake: dark chocolate matcha with berries. She knew she wanted a live band. *No DJs!* She had even selected a venue: the Huntley Hotel rooftop on Santa Monica Beach.

Before she graduated college, Heather had also chosen her groom-to-be. His name was Elliot. He came from a wealthy Pacific Palisades family and planned to join his father's commercial real estate development company.

But Elliot was a reluctant groom. He did not believe in marriage. Although he had seen his fair share of Hollywood romantic comedies, as a child of divorce, he knew the impermanence of marital unions.

Still, Heather was insistent. Their marriage would be different; she just knew it. They would beat the odds!

Still, Elliot was a practical young man. At his father's insistence, he told Heather the only way he'd agree to marry was if they first signed a prenuptial agreement.

Heather was floored. "That's the opposite of romantic!"

But Elliot said he had no choice. "If we marry without one, my dad will cut me out of his will."

This gave Heather pause. Yes, she was a romantic. But when it came to money matters, she could be just as practical as her fiancé.

So Heather agreed to hire an attorney. Over several meetings, she got a better sense of what marriage would entail and what would happen if she and Elliot parted ways.

Her rose-colored glasses gone, Heather now approached her upcoming marriage with the sober maturity such a monumental life change demands. For the first time, she saw beyond the pomp and pageantry of her "dream wedding" and considered the long-term demands and responsibilities of living as husband-and-wife.

The weight of the prenup appeared to have done its job, for more than fifteen years later, Heather and Elliot are still together—and the proud parents of two healthy girls. And I'm told she is already planning weddings for both.

> Prenups generally focus on financial payments, real and personal property, and other tangible assets, not on the roles and responsibilities of individuals in a marriage. While the terms "marriage contract," "marriage agreement," and "prenup" are sometimes interchangeable, the terms of formal prenups can be enforced by the courts.

There Is No Such Thing as a "Quickie" Divorce

Like any legal procedure, divorces require time. How much depends on the complexity of a couple's finances and the degree of enmity between litigants. In California, a "simple" no-fault divorce usually takes six months to complete. If the spouses are intent on making things hard for each other, the process can last years. I've even had clients who wanted me to stall the process just to stick it to their hated spouses.

Personally, I think their money could have been spent in better ways.

The Case of the Deferred Dissolution

Tad and Laura were in their twelfth year of marriage when "irreconcilable differences" prompted the pair to divorce. From the onset, it was clear this was not going to be a simple parting-of-the-ways. Tad owned a successful real estate development business as well as a twenty-eight-unit rental apartment complex and several smaller investment properties. They also had two grammar-school-aged daughters.

Everyone knew this divorce would take time. What no one could have guessed was how *much* time.

The first filings occurred in 2005. Tad, an astute businessman, made a generous initial offer of $11 million in cash and other assets. But Laura's lawyer was contentious and convinced her she could get more. After all, Tad's business was booming, and real estate prices were sky-high.

She responded by demanding $18 million.

Things went back and forth for three more years. Finally, in 2008, both sides prepared to go to court. We readied for a twenty-one-day-long trial. But the family court system was backed up and could not accommodate a trial of this length. The judge ordered a status conference during which we suggested ways to speed the proceedings—for three months hence. In the interim, we decided to hire a private judge and conduct the matter on our own terms.

But things were changing rapidly.

By this time, the Great Recession had hit like a wrecking ball. Tad's business was suddenly in decline, as were the value of his real estate holdings. Tad now had to pledge a substantial amount of assets for each of several developments he was building. He could make or lose up to $10 million with each job. Plus, the girls were getting older. They were now in high school, and their needs were different than they had been when this whole process began.

So back and forth things went. As negotiations dragged on, Tad's real estate business collapsed. He had to sell off his investment properties to avoid bankruptcy. Trying to determine the couple's net worth at this point was like trying to catch fireflies blindfolded.

Exhausted, Tad and Laura agreed to terms in early 2015. Total time elapsed: ten years. By now, the girls were in college. Custody was no longer an issue. As for the cash settlement, Laura walked away with $5 million, less than half of what she could have gotten a decade earlier.

(And this didn't account for inflation.) And her combined legal and accounting bill? North of $750,000.

The Rolling Stones may have sung "Time Is on My Side," but in a divorce, it rarely is.

Stage-of-Life Considerations

Age and family status can have a huge impact on divorce. While marrying young significantly increases the likelihood of divorce, youth also lessens the long-term trauma a divorce necessarily triggers. Someone who marries at eighteen and divorces at nineteen is basically calling a "mulligan"—a do-over—and will probably get on with life a bit sadder but also, one would hope, wiser.

By contrast, someone who marries at twenty-eight and, at forty, has two school-aged children, will find readjusting to singlehood more difficult. Dating can be uncomfortable for someone who's been "off the market" for a decade or more and who necessarily bears the scars of a failed long-term relationship. And if minor children are still in the picture, one is still not truly "single."

Finally, divorce among older working adults and even retirees brings a host of complications of its own, including the question: What now? While many older divorcees manage to find new partners, the prospect of another marriage is often no longer on the table because of potential problems with inheritances and Social Security payouts.

The Bottom Line

Divorce is little fun for anybody. Not even for the lawyers who get paid to facilitate it. (Hey, somebody's got to do it.) If you can find a way to avoid divorce, do it. Your children will thank you. Your blood pressure will thank you. Your bank account will be on its knees in gratitude.

But if divorce is your only option for regaining your safety, your sanity, and your self-respect, then it's time to bite the bullet and forge ahead armed with the knowledge and tools to make the process as painless as possible.

In the next chapter, we delve into what it takes to bring about that best possible outcome.

DIVORCE JOKE FOR THE ROAD

Two ninety-year-olds arrive in divorce court. The judge looks at the petition in front of him and then down at the wizened, stooped husband and wife.

"Um," the judge begins. "You two have been married for nearly seventy years. Why are you coming before me now?"

The silver-haired wife looks up at the judge, her mouth pursed. "Because, Your Honor. *Enough is enough!*"

2

I FEEL YOUR PAIN

Years ago, there was a TV commercial for a male hair restoration service called Hair Club for Men. The well-coiffed CEO, serving as company spokesman, ended each spiel with the now-famous line, "I'm not only the Hair Club president, but I'm also a client!"[1] In other words, having been bald, the guy had the bona fides to relate to his target market.

By that yardstick, I'm eminently qualified to speak about divorce law. I'm not only a well-educated, experienced, and successful divorce attorney—I'm also divorced. (No, I didn't represent myself in court. As the old saying goes, "Any lawyer who represents himself has a fool for a client.")

Like many modern divorces, mine was triggered by that old standby, "irreconcilable differences." As my wife and I matured, our interests, goals, and tastes diverged, while our tolerance for each other's habits, idiosyncrasies, and peccadillos diminished.

Ultimately, we agreed that, while difficult, being apart would still be easier than trying to live together. It took over a year to finalize the dissolution, including arranging custody for our two daughters, but once the deed was done, we were both happier for it. So, yeah, I've been there, done that. Divorce law isn't just my job. To me, it's personal.

A Short History of Divorce, Part 1: Ancient Egypt

As a legal concept, divorce appears to be nearly as old as the institution of marriage itself. It only makes sense that if people were going to invent a way to legally bind themselves to one another, they would also create an escape route.

> ### HUMOR HELPS!
>
> Divorce is serious business. But having a sense of humor can get you through it.
>
> I was once involved in a case where our evidence against the wife included a collection of not two, not three, but ten dildos. Large ones, too.
>
> When presented with these exhibits, the judge balked. "What am I supposed to do with these?"
>
> Everyone shifted uncomfortably. Finally, I raised my hand. "I'll take them, Your Honor." Everybody cracked up. Even the judge.
>
> No, I didn't actually take the dildos. But we did win the case.

The oldest divorce document on record dates from the reign of Ancient Egypt's Amasis II, who ruled from 570 to 526 BC during what we now call the Pharaonic Period. According to surviving papyrus records, a divorce could be requested by a husband or wife for one of several reasons:

- Adultery (by either party)

- Infertility (the wife was usually blamed)

- "Irreconcilable differences" (the two just hated each other)

To institute a divorce, a husband had to say, "I am leaving you," and then hand over a written document signed by four witnesses confirming the marriage was indeed over, and the wife was now free to marry another if she so chose.

Interestingly, by law, the husband had to provide his ex with spousal support, which tended to be a multiplier of the dowry he received at the marriage's onset. (In the Pharaonic period, this tended to be a factor of five, but it rose to a whopping ten during the later Ptolemaic period when divorce became less socially acceptable.)

Ancient Egyptian wives could also institute a divorce and, as in modern times, demand compensation from their exes while doing so. It may come as a surprise to many that Ancient Egyptian law gave women divorce *and* property rights comparable to those Western women enjoy today. However, to date, historians have found no surviving documentation regarding child support.

YEAH, BUT HE'S *MY* SON OF A B**CH

Fabled Brooklyn Dodgers manager Leo Durocher famously said, "Nice guys finish last." He was talking about baseball. But he might as well have been talking about law. Especially divorce law.

In divorce court, you want to be represented by an attorney who is smart, clever, knowledgeable, experienced, personable, and

continued

affable—but above all, when necessary, ruthless. To win in court, sometimes you must be mean. Sometimes you must ask pointed questions. Sometimes you must play hardball.

The key to being a good litigator? Knowing when to be an a**hole. I like to say, "You can't be an a**hole all the time. Or a son of a b**ch." You have to know when to turn it on and when to turn it off. Otherwise, you risk provoking judges and squandering opportunities to get the best divorce outcome.

I admit, when I'm representing a client, I can be a son of a b**ch. But if I'm your lawyer, I'll be your son of a b**ch. And that only works to your benefit.

A Short History of Divorce, Part 2: Ancient Rome

Compared to twenty-first century Americans, Ancient Romans had it rough. They had no motorized transportation. No antibiotics. No telephones. No air conditioning. No Netflix.

But one area where they had it easy was divorce. In Ancient Rome, marriage was not controlled by the government or the Church (because there *was* no Church). Marriage was simply a private agreement between a man and a woman.

In Rome's early years, the principal of *patria potestas* ("paternal power") meant men had total control over their wives as well as their children. If a husband wanted a divorce, he merely had to say so to his wife (in front of witnesses) or, if he wasn't into confrontation, he could just send her a letter.

And that was that.

Later, around 100 BC, women acquired the right to demand a divorce, too. There was no need to prove adultery, abuse, or other "wicked" behavior; it was simply "Arrivederci, baby," and she was outta there.

So you could say the Romans invented no-fault divorce.

While marital dissolution in Ancient Rome was easy, joint property disposition was another matter. For while Roman courts did not control marriage, they *did* have much to say when it came to property rights.

Under Roman law, if a couple split, the wife's dowry—or the cash equivalent thereof—went with her. (This allowed ex-wives to marry again if they so chose.) For this reason, Roman husbands usually kept their doweries sequestered from their other holdings; one never knew when it might become advantageous or necessary to forfeit these assets. The last thing a Roman patrician wanted was for his angry wife to demand her dowry back, and to then have to say, "Uh. Sorry, honey, but the funds are all tied up in aqueducts."

As for child custody, that was easy. The principle of *patria potestas* held fast until the fall of Rome, meaning the kids stayed with Dad. For this reason, many Roman women remained in unhappy marriages. They didn't want to lose their children.

Know the Players

Like any legal case, a divorce is very much a drama. And like any production, it has a cast of characters. Before entering this arena, it's key to know all the characters you're likely to encounter and what to expect.

The litigants. These are you and your (soon-to-be former) spouse. In this performance, you're the good guy, and your spouse is the bad guy. Still, you may wish to part ways on amicable terms. If you manage to do this, good for you. But things don't always go as planned. And if things get nasty, you must be prepared to go for the jugular.

Because divorces are considered civil cases—as opposed to criminal proceedings—a litigant is neither the *plaintiff* nor the *defendant*. The plaintiff may be called the *petitioner* and the defendant the *respondent*.

Traditionally, in civil cases, the plaintiff is the party claiming injury and seeking restitution, whereas the defendant is the party accused of causing the alleged injury. Likewise, the petitioner is the person seeking the divorce, whereas the respondent is the person from whom the divorce is being sought.

This all made sense when, to seek a divorce, one spouse had to accuse the other of adultery, abuse, or some other heinous transgression. But today, in states like California recognizing no-fault divorce, who is the plaintiff/petitioner and who is the defendant/respondent is rarely more than a matter of semantics. The plaintiff is simply the person who files first.

The attorneys. These are gladiators. The black knights. The contenders. Each has one and only one interest: to see that their client emerges with the best possible outcome. It's best to give them the freedom to do their jobs. To fight for you.

Although all attorneys receive the same general education and must pass their state bar to practice, most quickly gravitate to a specific area of the law. There are more than twenty specialties, ranging from animal law to tax law. For a divorce, you will want an attorney who specializes in *family law*.

In addition to divorce litigation and child custody disputes, family law may also cover such topics as adoption, surrogacy, and paternity. If you're seeking advice on wills and trusts, look for a lawyer who specializes in estate planning.

The judge. Divorce hearings are not jury trials. The trial is run—and decided—by a single person: the judge. Each judge comes to a case with their own personality, temperament, experience, expectations, demands, and prejudices. It's important that you and especially your attorney can "read" the judge and do what's necessary to get on their good side. Studies show if the judge likes you, they are more likely to rule in your favor.

In family law, a judge's two primary concerns are *justice* and *efficiency.* They want nothing more than for each warring couple to come to an equitable arrangement and take great care to see the interests of the children, if any, remain paramount. At the same time, with time and resources always at a premium, judges want things to move swiftly and have little patience for attorneys who are tardy, unprepared, or appear to intentionally stall the proceedings.

The good news is most of the judges I have argued before in Orange County are well-educated, experienced, even-tempered, impartial, compassionate, and pretty darned smart. I have also encountered a few who don't quite fit this description, but I won't name names as I might have to argue before them in the future.

The children. If you have kids, these are the innocent bystanders. You want to keep them as far away from the drama as possible to avoid collateral damage. This divorce is not their fault, and they should not have to suffer any more than they already have.

The experts. Most divorces, especially complex ones involving wealthy people, also involve testimony from outside experts. These may include forensic accountants, psychologists, and, in cases involving alleged domestic abuse, law enforcement officers. These witnesses may be hired by the litigants or be appointed by the court.

Along the expertise lines, in one unusual case I had, there was a dispute in which the husband insisted he owed his ex-wife nothing because they had never been legally married. In fact, he claimed their marriage had been a ruse, that he had never signed the proper legal registration form.

When the form in question was submitted into evidence, the man insisted his signature had been forged by someone else. This forced me to hire a well-known handwriting expert who could examine the signature and testify to its authenticity.

Turns out, the signature *was* genuine. The husband was legally married and so could now be legally divorced, with all that entailed.

A Short History of Divorce, Part 3: Medieval Europe

While Ancient Rome was quite liberal concerning divorce, its successor, medieval Europe, was just the opposite. By the second half of the first millennium AD, the Catholic Church had taken full control of the institution, transforming it from a private agreement to a holy sacrament. (When one got married, one did so not only before one's family, friends, and community but before God. And what God hath brought together, let no man put asunder.)

During the Middle Ages, there were only two ways for couples to end a marriage, and both were under the Church's purview. The first was an annulment. An annulment was an official decree that a marriage was null and void. In other words, it never really happened.

The most popular way to seek an annulment was to "discover" that husband and wife were actually related by blood. What constituted related by blood? That could shift from kingdom to kingdom.

Certainly, marriages between brothers and sisters were universally forbidden. (Ick.) Other jurisdictions frowned on unions of first and even second cousins. And, in others, up to seven degrees of separation was considered sufficient to declare incest. Of course, back then, with populations relatively small and the number of aristocrats particularly limited, being able to find common ancestors somewhere up any couple's family tree was relatively easy.

Another way to request an annulment? Declare the marriage had never been consummated. In other words, bride and groom never had sex. Because the Church saw procreation as marriage's key purpose, failure to get it on was clearly a legitimate justification for marital dissolution.

But how would one prove this? Either the wife had to demonstrate to authorities she was still a virgin (i.e., her hymen was intact) or the husband had to declare himself impotent. As either of these moves was clearly humiliating, most medieval couples looking to split took the incest route.

If, for whatever reason, the Church refused to issue an annulment, an unhappy couple had one more recourse: *divorce.* This was something the Church could not condone. (As stated earlier, the Church considered divorce to be sacrilegious.) Instead, the state itself would have to declare the marriage over—*by an act of the legislature.* Yes, in the Middle Ages, it took the medieval equivalent of an act of Congress to get a divorce.

It should also be noted that, in medieval times, both annulments and divorces were expensive. It helped to know the right people in the right places. Which is why divorces were mostly privileges of the top 1 percent. As for the average peasant, farmer, or tradesman? It was "'til death do us part."

A Short History of Divorce, Part 4: America

As the early American colonies were founded by either fortune hunters (Virginia) or religious devotees (New England), it's not surprising that, during the pre-Revolutionary era, divorce was a rarity in British North America.

The Puritans in the North had no tolerance for divorce. In the 1600s, perhaps one divorce was granted in all of Massachusetts and Connecticut during a given year. In the early mid-Atlantic colonies such as Virginia and the Carolinas, the lack of women made marriages rare enough. Divorces were even more so.

For the record, the first official divorce on American soil was that of Anne Clarke of the Massachusetts Bay Colony, who divorced her husband, Denis Clarke, on January 5, 1643. Denis admitted to abandoning his wife, with whom he had two children, to live with another woman, with whom he also fathered two kids.

After America gained independence, things changed rapidly. The same Enlightenment-fueled revolutionary fervor that had led the Thirteen Colonies to sever ties with the mother country triggered a similar drive for independence among its citizens. Unfortunately, states didn't begin collecting records of divorce until after the Civil War. But the statistics compiled in the second half of the nineteenth century reveal a clear upward trend in marriage dissolution (see Table 2.1).

Table 2.1. Percentage of US marriages ending in divorce

Years	Divorce rate
1867–1879	.03%
1880–1886	.04%
1887–1890	.05%
1891–1897	.06%
1898–1900	.07%

Source: US Department of Health, Education, and Welfare, "100 Years of Marriage and Divorce Statistics: United States, 1867–1967," December 1973, https://stacks.cdc.gov/view/cdc/12831.

To satisfy a growing demand for quick and painless divorces, many "divorce mills" were established around the country, principally in the frontier states and territories of the West and Midwest. During the mid-eighteenth century, perhaps the most notorious of these was Indiana, where judges were glad to grant divorces to anyone who could "prove residence" and a "statutory cause" by which a divorce could be granted.[2]

Proving residence was simple: as Indiana had no residency requirements at the time, all one had to do was provide an address. (It could even be a hotel.) As for a statutory requirement, this was generally interpreted to be any reason a judge deemed proper, such as the married couple no longer wished to stay together.

Under increasing public pressure, many of the so-called divorce mills tightened their requirements by the beginning of the twentieth century. One notable exception was Nevada, which was famously the go-to state for couples seeking a "quickie" divorce prior to the 1960s. In the early twentieth century, the city of Reno became the hub of an entire divorce industry operating with the cool efficiency of a Detroit assembly line.

Here was the formula for getting a "Reno Divorce":

1. Either the husband or wife would call a Reno-based divorce attorney to retain his services.

2. The spouse would then travel to Reno (usually by car or train, as this was before the era of affordable commercial air travel) where he or she would be met by the attorney or his assistant.

3. The spouse would then be put up at a local hotel (at their expense), which would serve as his or her "residence."

4. The attorney would serve a summons on the other spouse, specifying a date and time for his or her court appearance.

5. Under Nevada law, anyone seeking a divorce had to live in the state for six weeks and was forbidden to leave for more than twenty-four hours at a time. This was, for most people, the hard part of securing a "quickie" divorce and was often jokingly called "doing time" in Reno.

6. At the appointed hour, the spouse and his or her attorney would arrive in court. The other side was not required to show up; assigning another local lawyer to serve as representation was sufficient. At the judge's direction, the plaintiff would then offer a reason for requesting the divorce—"irreconcilable differences" was considered sufficient. A witness (usually hired by the attorney) would confirm that one spouse had satisfied Nevada's residency requirements. This person would then swear he or she had the intention of becoming a permanent Nevada resident, and the divorce would be granted. This whole appearance usually took all of five minutes, after which the now ex-spouse was free to go his or her merry way. Free at last.

Of course, spending six weeks in Reno, Nevada, is probably not what most people would consider quick, but it was certainly shorter than the six *months* or more other states required (and many still do) before getting a divorce. As it turns out, Reno's divorce industry was hit hard when in 1969, neighboring California, under then-Governor Ronald Reagan, passed the nation's first no-fault divorce legislation. No longer was it required to prove adultery, battery, mental cruelty, or other offenses to secure a divorce.

As in Nevada, "irreconcilable differences" were sufficient. Many states quickly followed suit. Today, seventeen states offer no-fault divorces. In addition to California, these are Colorado, Florida, Hawaii,

Indiana, Iowa, Kansas, Kentucky, Michigan, Minnesota, Missouri, Montana, Nebraska, Nevada, Oregon, Washington, and Wisconsin.

Today, the divorce rate nationwide hovers between 45 and 50 percent, where it has been for the last thirty years. However, the *number* of divorces is actually declining. This is due to fewer couples getting married. The one demographic in which divorces continue to climb is among couples fifty and older. The so-called gray divorce rate doubled between 1990 and 2010.

MORE ON "FAMILY LAW"

Family law in the United States has evolved significantly over the decades. When our country was founded, most laws regarding marriage, divorce, and related matters were based on English common law, which tended to weigh heavily in favor of men.

Things began to change in the mid-nineteenth century when women acquired a limited number of property rights and again in the early twentieth century when they won the vote. Laws regarding spousal support, aka alimony, advanced significantly beginning in the 1970s, and by the early twenty-first century, ideas about *who* one could marry—let alone divorce—began to include same-sex couples.

One thing about family law that has *not* changed over the years is that, for the most part, specific rules and regulations have remained the province of individual states. (The Supreme Court ruling in *Obergefell v. Hodges* in 2015, which established the legality of same-sex marriage nationwide, being a notable exception.) However, federal laws require marriages and divorces in each state be recognized by all other states.

continued

> So, if you get married in New York, divorced in California, and remarried in Kansas, you can't be charged with bigamy if you move to Illinois.

The Divorce That Changed History

Arguably, no divorce in history has had as much impact on Western culture than that of England's King Henry VIII and his first wife, Catherine of Aragon.

In 1501, the rival kingdoms of England and Spain tried to form an alliance by marrying King Henry VII's eldest son and heir apparent, Prince Arthur, to Katherine of Aragon, scion of one of Spain's most wealthy, powerful families. At the time they were wed, both Arthur and Katherine were all of fifteen years old. Just one year later, the young prince died of a malady then called "sweating sickness," now believed to be a form of the rat-borne hantavirus, leaving Katherine a widow and Arthur's younger brother, Henry, next in line for the throne.

In 1509, King Henry VII died, and Prince Henry became Henry VIII, the new monarch. That same year, Henry married his late brother's widow, Katherine of Aragon, for whom he had long pined, making her once again Queen of England. Because guaranteeing succession was any medieval royal's first priority, Henry and Katherine got to work producing a male heir.

And this is where things started to go south. Over the next few years, Katherine had five children, all of whom were either stillborn or who died shortly after childbirth. Only her last child, a girl, whom they named Mary, survived.

Henry was not pleased.

He was determined to have a *male* heir, something Katherine appeared incapable of producing. Enter Anne Boleyn, daughter of a wealthy English family and one of Queen Katherine's ladies in waiting. A beautiful, clever, and ambitious young woman, Anne worked her way into King Henry's heart—not to mention his pants—convincing the king she could produce the male heir he was so determined to sire. She even managed to get herself impregnated while Henry was still wed to Katherine.

To make his coming heir legitimate, Henry had to marry Anne. Fast. Which meant he first had to dump Katherine. But as both Henry and Katherine were Catholic, a divorce was impossible.

But Henry *could* request an annulment. He did so, appealing directly to Pope Clement VII, arguing he had displeased God by marrying his brother's widow. The Pope didn't buy it. Such a marriage is actually *encouraged* in the Old Testament (Deuteronomy 25:5–10) and thus proclaimed their marriage both legitimate and permanent.

Frustrated, Henry then asked the Pope for a *dispensation.* This meant that, while divorce was *verboten* for everyone else, it was okay for Henry because he was a *king*.

Still, Clement said, "No! No divorce for you." (Reminiscent of the Soup Nazi in *Seinfeld*.)

At this, Henry flew into a rage—*he was the king of England, dammit!*—and, in a fit of pique, withdrew all of England from the Catholic Church and formed a church of his own: The Church of England! With him as its head. (Hey, if Martin Luther could defy Rome, he could, too!)

And, as the head of his church, Henry could grant himself a divorce. Which is exactly what he did. (Via the compliant Archbishop of Canterbury.) He married Anne in a secret ceremony and later introduced her to the world as his new queen in a lavish coronation procession.

For all intents and purposes, the new Church of England was traditional Catholicism, but with its pope in London, not Rome. Which suited Henry just fine.

Not surprisingly, the British Catholic Church establishment was not particularly happy with this new branding. It owned approximately one-third of all the land in England. And it was still fiercely loyal to the Pope. This made it a direct threat to Henry. So, to preserve his new marriage and the legitimacy of his coming heir, Henry set about dissolving the churches, abbeys, monasteries, and other Church holdings throughout England and claiming them for himself. Many heads were lost in the process. Literally.

As for Anne Boleyn, she produced a girl: Elizabeth. Henry's plan hadn't gone quite as anticipated. So they got back at it. Anne had two more babies, both of whom were stillborn. Shortly thereafter, Anne was charged with incest, witchcraft, adultery, and treason against the king and beheaded.

Damn. And you thought *your* divorce was rough.

The Need for Speed

The faster a divorce can be settled, the better it is for everyone. It's better not only for your bank account but also for your peace of mind. There are three ways to speed up the process.

Quickly assemble all the relevant documentation. As part of the divorce process, you'll be asked to complete what's called a Preliminary Declaration of Disclosure. This includes a complete schedule of assets and debts, income and expenses, and any supporting documentation, such as tax returns, bank statements, investment statements, and so on. If there's a prenuptial agreement, you definitely want to include that, too.

Hire your experts early. Determine what evidence you will need to make your case, and then secure the services of high-quality third-party experts to testify on your behalf. Why is time an issue? First, leading authorities are always in demand. The people you want may not be available when you need them, so the sooner you start your search, the more time you have to find credible substitutes, if necessary. Second, it may take time for your experts to sift through all the available information. This is particularly true when talking about forensic accountants. A rushed analysis is likely to be incomplete, if not erroneous. Finally, there are only so many top experts to go around, and you want to snag the stars before the other side does!

Propose a settlement. Know in advance what you want to get out of the divorce and put it in writing. Be specific. Think: House. Business. Vehicles. Investments. If you have children, what should the custody arrangement be? Include an argument supporting your case, especially if any of your requests may seem one-sided.

THE MOST EXPENSIVE DIVORCE IN HISTORY

By far the most expensive divorce in history was the 2019 split of Amazon founder Jeff Bezos and his then-wife, Mackenzie Scott Bezos. As part of their settlement, Mackenzie received a 4 percent stake in Amazon, at the time worth $38 billion. That's ten times more than the total value of the second-most-expensive

continued

divorce, that of French American businessman and art dealer Alec Wildenstein and his wife, Jocelyn, whose 1999 settlement topped out at "just" $3.8 billion.

So, you've decided that despite all the pain you may endure, divorce *is* your best option. So be it. It's time to discover how the process works here in California and what you must do to make sure you come out on top.

3

PLANNING IS EVERYTHING

The general who wins the battle makes many calculations in his temple before the battle is fought. The general who loses makes but few calculations beforehand.

—Sun-Tzu, *The Art of War*

If you fail to plan, you are planning to fail.

—Attributed to Benjamin Franklin

War is hell. So is divorce.

And both take great care and planning if a campaign is to succeed. To prepare for a divorce, you would do well to think of it as mortal combat. Certainly, the remainder of your life—and your ability to enjoy that life—hangs on the outcome.

To prevail, you must, like any great general, know your adversary's strengths, weaknesses, goals, and vulnerabilities. You must also anticipate their likely moves well in advance, prepare your defenses, and, if needed, ready your counterattack. Build your arsenal—records, documents, deeds, testimonials, and so on—until you feel they represent an overwhelming force.

Then prepare to move swiftly and decisively. The longer your battle lasts, the greater the chances unpredictable events will appear to trip you up. Unlike a fine wine, a divorce does not get better with age.

Yours, Mine, and Ours

California is one of only nine "community property" states in the United States. (The others are Arizona, Idaho, Louisiana, Nevada, New Mexico, Texas, Washington, and Virginia.) Knowing this, you must plan your divorce accordingly.

Under community property provisions, virtually all assets and income a couple acquires and/or earns during a marriage, as well as debts incurred, is owned *jointly*. In the event of divorce, these assets are split fifty-fifty. When it comes to a fixed asset, like a house or car, that cannot be divided, either the asset will be sold and the resulting monies split equally, or one party will take possession and the other will be awarded cash or property of equal value.

But not all property held by a couple is necessarily *community* property. Even in states like California, courts also recognize the presence of *separate* property. This is defined as the following:

- Any asset owned *prior* to the marriage (e.g., a business, your collection of classic Beatles albums, etc.)

- Any asset acquired during the marriage by way of inheritance or gift as it is defined by the California Family Code

- Assets/earnings acquired post-separation

Business Valuation Considerations

A common issue in divorce in OC is where one spouse has a premarital business. During marriage, the business value may have substantially increased. Absent a prenup agreement, the court will utilize one of two methods (Pereira or Van Camp) to determine whether or not the community has gained a financial interest in the separate property business.

Let's discuss both now.

The Pereira Method

This is the method courts most commonly use when a piece of separate property—for example, a small business—increases in value mostly because of one spouse's investment of time, skill, and effort. (This distinguishes it from value increases resulting from *outside* market forces, like inflation; the adoption of new, readily available tech; market trends; etc.)

Note: The court determines a separate property's value based on when an asset was acquired and then attributes a fair rate of return on that asset over the course of the marriage. (Usually, something shy of the legal interest rate—currently 10 percent—calculated annually. The Pereira Court uses 7 percent, but each court is free to use something different.) Any remainder is considered community property.

The Van Camp Method

Sometimes, a piece of separate property's value can increase substantially through no direct effort of its owner. For example, a painting, a rare coin collection, or a piece of real estate can appreciate markedly merely because of market trends and speculation. Even a business can find its value balloon merely because it happens to be in the right place at the right time. Or because of the contributions of people *other* than its owner.

If You've Always Wanted to Be James Bond, Here's Your Chance to Act like a Super Spy

It's one thing to claim something is separate property and quite another to prove it in court. To do this, you must "bring the receipts." In other words, provide convincing documentation. If you can't establish a watertight paper trail yourself, you may have to hire the services of a specialist, like a forensic accountant. This can be expensive, so it's best that you compile as much documentation as early as possible.

This can prove tricky, especially if your spouse realizes you are contemplating divorce (even if you're not *yet*).

In the movies, intelligence agents use all kinds of tricks and gadgets to acquire, transmit, and protect sensitive information. Over the years, microfilm cameras, hollow boot heels, and autokey ciphers have given way to button cameras, thumb drives, and digital encryption.

When compiling documentation prior to a divorce, you need not be as crafty as an international spook, but you do need to be thorough. And discreet. Ways to protect your records and receipts include:

- Collecting your critical files and then emailing them to yourself

- Keeping files electronically in more than one place

- Putting records in a document vault (e.g., your Android/Apple backup)

- Keeping physical copies in a physical safe

- Using double authentication/encryption

- Employing blockchain technology for data storage

Also, don't merely rely on banks and other financial institutions to do your work for you. By law, such institutions are required to keep records for only seven years. If your marriage lasts longer than that, records of your original transactions will likely have been destroyed.

Planning *Does* Pay Off

Billy and Bonnie married in 1999, a year after I began practicing law. Right away, the two had marital problems. Bonnie didn't trust Billy. He gambled. He made huge purchases without asking her. He had a roving eye.

Bonnie was naturally concerned.

The prior year, she had started her own floral business using $20,000 she had saved during college. She worried that, should she and Billy divorce, Billy would take half.

Even in those days, I told my clients to document all their business activities and warned Bonnie of serious consequences if she did not. Fortunately, Bonnie followed my instructions. Year after year, she digitally sent me her business financials, including tax returns and bank statements. She never told Billy any of this.

What Billy did know? They rented a safe deposit box where his wife kept valuable papers.

In the mid-2000s, it was clear their marriage was over. By then, Bonnie's chain of flower shops was estimated to be worth $4 million. Thinking he was clever, Billy went to the bank, accessed the safe deposit box, removed all of Bonnie's papers, and burned them. (He figured that if the records didn't exist, it would be her word against his, and he'd get half her assets.)

He had not counted on me having backup copies to the files. In court, we proved the business began with Bonnie's seed money, was hers alone, and that the shop's success was the result of her efforts. Our forensic accountant was then able to conduct the typical Pereira or Van Camp analysis despite Billy's shenanigans.

What the Three Little Pigs Can Teach Us about Planning

Once upon a time, there were three little pigs. All got married. Then all filed for divorce. And all were hoping to avoid trial by settling out of court.

The first little piggy didn't make any plans. He didn't take a deposition. He didn't do discovery. He didn't do a business valuation or a vocational evaluation or a child custody evaluation. Instead, he just hoped it would all work out with a fat settlement check. Unsurprisingly, this "house of straw" blew away at the first stiff wind, and he had to go to trial.

The second little piggy wasn't lazy or complacent. She just wasn't proactive. She waited too long to hire experts. She didn't do due diligence when it came to a vocational evaluation and didn't get the child custody evaluation in time for it to make a difference. This "house of sticks" proved to be an easy pushover, the resulting trial costing her all the time and money she hoped to save.

The third little piggy was on the case from day one. He was aggressively proactive. In a timely fashion, he executed:

- Discovery
- Deposition

- Cash flow analysis

- Subpoenas

- Business valuation

- Vocational evaluation

- Child custody evaluation

Not only did this "house of bricks" help him avoid trial, but his ex agreed to settle early for an amount he could easily live with.

Plan for Divorce Before—and After—Your Wedding

To many people, planning for divorce sounds like you're setting yourself up for failure. The old self-fulfilling prophesy. But it's also being realistic. As we discuss in Chapter 1, odds are your marriage *won't* survive "'til death do you part." And as another adage suggests, "Hope for the best; prepare for the worst." If things should go south, it's best you're prepared. In writing.

Preparation can therefore be of enormous help when it comes time to differentiate separate from community property. In such an event, one of three common scenarios is likely to occur.

Scenario 1: A Prenup Is in Place

In this situation property division is specified in writing before the wedding, making any subsequent property division clear and uncontestable.

Example: Brenda's dad gave her $300,000 when she turned twenty-one. One year later, when preparing to marry Alvin, her college sweetheart, Brenda signed a prenup stating this $300,000 was, in fact, hers. Soon after the couple wed, Brenda used this money for down payment on a house. Fifteen years and three houses later, Brenda and Alvin divorced. Since they had a prenup, there was no debate: they would sell the house, Brenda would take $300,000 off the top, and the couple would split the remaining proceeds fifty-fifty.

Scenario 2: There Is a Postnup

A postnup, short for postnuptial agreement, is like a classic prenup, only it's drafted and signed *after* a couple is wed. Their purposes are the same: to lay out clearly the ownership of separate property in a divorce.

Example: After a few years of marriage, Brenda finds out that Alvin has been cheating on her. Brenda and Alvin wanted to remain together despite the infidelity. One caveat: Brenda insisted they both sign a postnup agreement, describing their rights and financial obligations to one another should the marriage dissolve. Upon divorce, the postnup established that Alvin would get 100 percent of the stock in his company. She would get 100 percent of the house and most of the cash. At the time of the divorce, the stocks happened to be worth ten times what she received. Some might think this to be unfair. Yet the court viewed it as they both got what they bargained for—that is, what they established in writing in their postnup, which held up in court.

Scenario 3: There Is No Prenup or Postnup

Absent a prenup or postnup, all property acquired is presumed to be community. If one wishes to establish separate property, the legal burden falls on them to prove it. This requires the expertise of a forensic accountant, often at great cost.

Example: Brenda's dad gives her $300,000 when she turns twenty-one, which she used as a down payment on their first house. After fifteen years of marriage, Brenda and Alvin decide to divorce. Naturally, Brenda wants her $300,000 back. But she has no record of the gift coming from her father; he's dead, and what records she had are gone.

It is her legal burden to prove that the contribution to the home came from her father, which she cannot do other than through her testimony. If the judge believes her, she could get the money. If he doesn't, she doesn't get the money.

Unfortunately, this last scenario is the most common. And it doesn't always have a happy ending. The more time has passed, the harder it can be to establish ownership of separate property in a way that satisfies a court of law. Which is why I always advise my clients to get a prenup or, if they are already married, create a postnup that lays this all out.

If you don't, you could be in for a world of pain.

The Case of the Lavish Landscaper

Tom and Evelyn were married for ten years. He was a high-earning investment banker. She owned a modestly successful landscape design business but, at age forty-five, recently retired.

I represented Tom. At issue now was the question of spousal support, which would necessarily be a function of the couple's standard of living.

On the witness stand, Evelyn testified she had quit her business because it was too hard on her body and back. I found it curious that she had made this move so soon after separating from Tom. It was as if she was *anticipating* being cared for with support and no obligation to earn on her own.

In her testimony, Evelyn made every effort to impress the judge with how Tom had spoiled her during the marriage. "He bought me a $10,000 Cartier watch," she noted, flashing the gold trinket on her wrist. "I had an unlimited budget for clothes at all the best boutiques."

Under cross-examination, I repeated her testimony back to her. "That's a nice dress," I noted, indicating her designer couture. "Was that expensive?"

She nodded, adding she bought it at one of Las Vegas's high-end malls.

"How much did it cost?"

"Six thousand dollars."

I then asked about her jewelry, which she identified as Bulgari. "How much for that?"

"Six to ten thousand dollars."

I then asked about her hair. "How often did you get it styled?"

"Twice a week. $250 per visit. Plus, I'd add another $150 for a mani-pedi once a week. And $325 every few months for Botox."

The costs were really adding up.

"What kind of shoes are you wearing?" I asked.

She stood up, bent down, and took off one of her six-inch high heels to show the judge. "Jimmy Choo," she said proudly.

"And where'd you get them?"

"Another high-end boutique."

And then she made her mistake. Still standing, she slipped her shoes back on in a move worthy of an Olympic gymnast.

The female judge looked at me like, "Are you effing kidding me?"

I had played into Evelyn's conceit, distracting her so she'd make her fatal error. After all, a big part of her case was predicated on the claim she was no longer physically capable of work. Yet, on the stand, her display of physical prowess clearly contradicted her disability claims, thus calling the rest of her testimony into question. As a result, the judge ruled favorably toward my client.

If Evelyn wished to continue living "in the style to which she had grown accustomed," she would have to do it on her own.

Why You Should Make Your Highest, Best Offer Early: A Cautionary Tale

When preparing for a divorce, doing your due diligence early can give you a good idea of what constitutes a realistic settlement offer. The first offer proffered is often the best you will get, so you must be able to recognize a generous proposal when it comes your way.

Granted, accepting an initial settlement offer runs contrary to everything we've ever been taught about negotiating. In most lawsuits, defendants tend to lowball their plaintiffs, hoping to settle quickly and save as much money as possible. As a result, plaintiffs are almost always advised to reject initial offers. But a divorce is different from your typical civil action.

In a divorce:

- The litigants know each other intimately, which makes subterfuge difficult.

- One spouse may feel guilty and make an offer that's significantly more generous than what could come from full-blown litigation. Such offers tend to get worse, not better, if rejected.

- Couples are usually eager to wrap things up as quickly as possible. (Think opportunity costs.) They know that long, drawn-out divorces benefit no one but the lawyers.

When *Can* a Divorce Be Simple?

Sometimes you can avoid a lot of pain—saving time and money—by being proactive in a different way. Imagine this scenario: A husband and wife are both W-2 wage earners. Neither owns a business. Neither is a stay-at-home spouse. If both are willing to be proactive and subscribe to the "present the highest and best offer early" strategy, they don't need the services of forensic accountants, much less child custody experts.

Let me tell this story in a different way:

Jack and Jill awake daily at dawn. Every morning, they go up the hill to fetch their pails of W-2 wages. At night they both come down the hill to relieve their son's nanny from her duties and get Chinese takeout. One day, Jack falls down and breaks his crown—and Jill does not come running after.

So Jack knows he needs a divorce.

Jack and Jill have led a simple life until now and can enjoy an equally simple divorce. Jack can say to his lawyer, "We have a $2 million house, $5 million in our 401(k)s, and $3 million in stocks."

With this in mind, Jack's attorney can make his highest and best offer. "Dear Jill's attorney," he can write. "For a complete settlement, we would like to sell the house and split the funds, divide the 401(k) equally, and divide the $1.5 million in stocks. Also, we'd like to equally share Little Jackie each week. We think we can live happily ever after so long as we can keep our own pail."

A simple tale with a simple ending.

And there you have a *simple* divorce, all because one took the pro-active approach of accepting the highest/best offer right out of the gate.

In this chapter, we've discussed the importance of planning your divorce—and planning early. We've also explored the concepts of separate and community property, spousal support, child support, and how smart planning can help you avoid going to trial.

Of course, you must keep in mind that no matter how simple and straight-forward you try to make it, a divorce is a legal proceeding. And this requires the participation of legal counsel. As with all things in life, divorce attorneys are not created equal. The *quality* of the lawyer you retain is likely to majorly affect the quality of your impending divorce settlement.

So let's now take a look at how to go about picking a lawyer who'll kick ass—er—I mean get you the best possible outcome.

4

HOW TO CHOOSE YOUR
ATTORNEY (WISELY)

I t's often said juries don't make decisions based on the facts of a
case; they simply vote on who they believe hired the best lawyer. Of
course, divorces don't go before juries. They're argued before judges.
Just the same, divorce settlements often come down to which side has
the best legal representation. Which is why choosing your family law
attorney may be one of the most important decisions you'll ever make.

I like to tell my clients that, when it comes to hiring a divorce
attorney, the relationship you're getting into is a lot like the relationship you're get out *of*. It's a partnership. An intimate one. In many
ways, even *more* intimate than an actual marriage. Hell, you'll tell your
divorce lawyer things you'd *never* consider admitting to your spouse.
(Unless you wanted a divorce.)

Now typically, when you are courting a prospective romantic mate,
there's a *process* involved: you date, you meet the other person's friends
and parents, you spend extended time together, you propose, you plan
the wedding.

Well, something analogous happens here. In the spirit of supporting your new union, here are the steps you should take to create and sustain your "new partnership."

Step 1: Search, Search, Search

People seeking a significant other have many ways to find the perfect match. They can let friends, family, and even associates know they are "looking" and request referrals. They can sign up with online dating sites or use a "swipe right" dating app. They can join groups to meet like-minded members of the opposite (or same) sex. In some "traditional" cultures, they can get help from a professional matchmaker.

People have similar options for finding a good divorce lawyer. They can ask friends, family members, and coworkers for referrals, especially if any of these folks have already gone through a divorce. They can also do an online search. (Google "best divorce lawyers near me" and you'll find many names.)

My advice?

Talk to your business attorney, financial advisor, or your CPA to discern who is the best person to represent your financial and family interests. Don't ask your hairdresser or your barber. You have too much at stake here, and your credentialed advisors likely have access to top lawyers you can trust.

Yet even if you get a glowing recommendation, how do you know this lawyer will be right for *you*?

Step 2: Get Third-Party Validation

Back in the Dark Ages—we're talking pre-internet—people had to take strangers at pretty much face value. All you could know about someone you just met is what they chose to tell you, or what information mutual friends felt comfortable sharing. (Not all of which could be trusted.)

If you were really paranoid about someone, you could hire a private investigator to dig into their background, but that was (and still is) *pricey*. Today, most everyone's personal details are there for the asking. Social media and web searches can reveal most of a person's life history, including a criminal record. Like it or not, there's little about someone that can't be uncovered with just a few mouse clicks.

Qualifications you can quickly ascertain online include:

- *Education.* From where did this attorney get their law degree?

- *Experience.* How many years has this attorney been practicing?

- *Specialty.* Does this attorney specialize in family law?

- *Associations.* Of what professional groups or organizations is this attorney a member?

Likewise, you can check the reputation and ratings for divorce attorneys much in the same way you might assess Yelp ratings for a local restaurant. (You also want to temper these searches with trusted credentials, as well as employing more stringent standards.) But be warned: opposing attorneys who've had their butts kicked can surreptitiously go on Yelp or Google, posing as a client and say nasty things about other lawyers with little or no consequence. That's why you really need to do your homework.

The following are some sites that review lawyers.

Martindale-Hubbel

America's oldest legal rating and review service. Founded in 1868, it offers peer-reviewed ratings for more than one million attorneys worldwide.

I hold an AV Preeminent rating with Martindale-Hubbel, the highest possible rating for both legal ability and ethical standards. In 2021 and 2022, I was given an AV Preeminent rating with Martindale-Hubbel in the Judicial Edition, reflecting the confidential opinions of members of both the bar and the judiciary. See https://www.martindale.com/.

AVVO

A relatively new service, it became part of Internet Brands, the same holding company that also owns Martindale-Hubble, in 2018. Despite its relative youth, the site has a strong reputation for depth and honesty in its attorney reviews. You can read here what AVVO says about me: https://www.avvo.com/attorneys/92660-ca-paul-nelson-145238.html.

Super Lawyers

This is yet another relatively new but nonetheless well-respected legal review service. In its own words, it rates "outstanding lawyers from more than seventy practice areas who have attained a high degree of peer recognition and professional achievement." In the years 2021, 2022, and 2023, I was recognized as a "Super Lawyer" in family law. You can find my review at this address: https://profiles.superlawyers.com/california-southern/newport-beach/lawyer/paul-nelson/e99525b1-36e6-4605-8bcf-5b2538f842d5.html.

Step 3: Make Sure You Have Strong Chemistry

What looks good on paper doesn't always pan out in real life. As with romantic partners, the quality of a lawyer-client relationship often comes down to personal compatibility more than some mathematical algorithm. An attorney may have a solid track record, a long list of professional citations, and a five-star rating from every review service, but if that spark isn't there, the relationship may not work. Don't fall into the trap of suffering a rocky start but hanging on in the hope things will improve. They probably won't.

So, what can you do to establish good relations with a prospective attorney? Above all, share your vision of how this divorce should go. How long do you think the process will take? What should the financial settlement be? If children are involved, how should custody be handled? Beyond this, how many other clients is this attorney currently representing? Can they give you the personal attention you desire, or will you be handed off to an associate? In the end, how do you *feel* about this person? Are you comfortable with them? Do you feel they can be trusted? Do you laugh at the same jokes?

If the vibe is a good one, you've likely found yourself a winner. If you're seeing red flags, if warning bells are going off, then it's probably best to continue searching.

Have I ever been rejected by a potential client? Absolutely. (And don't trust lawyers who say they haven't.) Some find me too aggressive. Others don't find me aggressive enough. Some people want me to do things I believe are unethical, and I tell them so. Some people think I'm just too damned expensive.

Conversely, I confess I've turned down clients who wish to hire me. If you have a simple divorce, I may not be the guy for you. If you have a modest net worth, yours is not a case I'm best positioned to handle. (Just as you don't go to a world-class brain surgeon for an annual check-up, you shouldn't approach a top-tier Newport Beach divorce attorney if you're a $70,000-dollar-a-year wage earner living in a two-bedroom rental with a spouse who makes extra money selling on Etsy.) Not that your divorce doesn't deserve professional attention—it most certainly does—but there are plenty of quality lawyers better suited to your needs and your pocketbook than someone like me.

Step 4: Determine Finances

Normally, when you get together with a future partner, you discuss personal finances (i.e., what are your individual assets and debts, how's your credit, how might you share costs as well as a checking account, etc.). Well, the same kind of reckoning should go into assessing how much you expect to pay for your divorce. The first thing you should ask upon learning your prospective lawyer's rate: Is the juice worth the squeeze?

Clients always have questions about total costs and hourly rates. Here are a few things to keep in mind:

- Attorney's rates are determined by their experience, their expertise, and their track record of success in litigation/court. Attorneys who are in high demand are likely to cost more than those who are not.

- Attorneys are typically paid by the hour, plus charge for any expenses they incur on your behalf. As of this writing, hourly rates for lawyers in California range from approximately $400 to $800 per hour. (If you have a high-value case, be prepared to pay at the high end.) Most family law attorneys will also demand a $7,500 to $25,000 retainer, which is an up-front payment against which subsequent hours will be charged.

- Rates don't equal final costs. Just because you have an attorney with a higher hourly rate doesn't mean you will pay more overall. Conversely, the same is true; an attorney billing a low hourly rate doesn't mean you will save money in the end. Lacking knowledge and/or expertise, a cut-rate attorney may have to do more research and go down several blind alleys before bringing your case to conclusion.

As stated previously, I am what most would call a "high-priced" lawyer, but my expensive expertise can save my clients money. Over the years, I have gone up against dozens of "discount" lawyers who just didn't understand marital math; because of these lawyer's ignorance and/or inexperience, I was able to negotiate settlements that put hundreds of thousands of extra dollars in my clients' pockets. Yes, I was paid handsomely for my services, but I think my clients would describe this as a wise investment. As for their exes, they paid less—and received far less as a result.

Overall, the adage holds true: you get what you pay for.

Step 5: Set Expectations

Before tying the proverbial knot, savvy couples share expectations concerning what they hope their union will achieve and the role each will play in it. Such expectations are ultimately expressed in the traditional marriage vows, usually a variation of the following:

I, _____, take you, _____, for my lawful wife/husband, to have and to hold from this day forward, for better, for worse, for richer, for poorer, in sickness and in health, until death do us part. I will love and honor you all the days of my life.

Strange as it may sound, the same dynamic is a good way to imagine your divorce attorney-client relationship. First, both sides must set expectations. In fact, if I had my way, both lawyer and client would recite vows before formalizing their business relationship. Attorneys, being ethically bound to put their clients' interests above their own, would say something like this:

Lawyer Vows

- I vow to zealously and effectively advocate for your position with the court and opposing counsel.

- I vow to maintain confidentiality 'til death do I part. *Never* will I share your confidences/secrets.

- I vow to interact with opposing counsel in a dignified, yet assertive manner.

- I vow to provide direct and unambiguous advice using my experience and expertise when counseling you.

- I vow to take reasonable legal positions based on the law as it is or as it should be.

In turn, clients would respond in kind, making themselves accountable for their actions and decisions. Here's how their vows might read:

Client Vows

- I vow to be honest with my attorney.
- I vow to collect and share information with my attorney.
- I vow to represent myself respectfully in court.
- I vow to adhere to behavioral instructions in and out of court.
- I vow to be responsive to requests from my attorney.

Should both sides respect their vows, they will likely live happily ever after. Or at least until the case closes.

Divorce Lawyers: The Best of Enemies?

It was the Old Testament that introduced the Devil to Western civilization. But he wasn't called the Devil. He was called Satan. And, curiously enough, he first appears as a "heavenly prosecutor," a subordinate to Yahweh (God), who prosecuted the nation of Judah in the Court of Heaven. In other words, *the Devil was a lawyer*.

Another interesting fact: Although we now think of the Devil as an enemy of God, the Hebrew *ha-satan* (the Satan) translates to modern English not as "enemy" but as "adversary." There's a key difference. An enemy is out to destroy you. An adversary simply wants to make things difficult for you to come out on top.

Importantly, adversaries can be opposed to each other, yet still get along. Think about any sports competition. Each team wants to outperform the other, not destroy them. (If destruction was the object of competition, professional sports couldn't exist.) At the end of a game, it's not uncommon for opposing players to even go out drinking together.

The same holds true for divorce lawyers. We are adversaries, *not* enemies. Our goal is to come out on top for our client, not destroy the other side. Like professional athletes, we must return to the same stadium (the courtroom) week after week, year after year, often encountering the same opponents and facing the same referees (judges).

Many of our greatest victories don't even take place in court. They're done in private conference rooms where we hash out deals behind closed doors. It's therefore incumbent on us to be civil. To be trustworthy. To even be friendly *and* accommodating.

Yes, I will serve as your loyal champion, but not at the cost of my own future or reputation. I will not take a ridiculous position with the judge, no matter how strongly you demand I do. I also will not bring up your spouse's infidelity just to feed your desire for revenge. (Besides, California is a no-fault state; in court, infidelity is a nonissue.) My job is to argue the facts of your case *within the law*, not to serve as an agent of vengeance.

I say this here to set expectations. After all, you will have but one divorce (hopefully). But I must live on to fight another day.

What You Must Understand about Lawyers

Here's an uncomfortable truth about lawyers: we're sophists. That is, we're perfectly capable of arguing both sides of any argument. This is not just by temperament but by training. We're taught to look at cases not in terms of right and wrong, but of weak and strong. Our goal is to *win*. And if we can't do that, it's to get the best possible resolution for our clients.

While our sophistry might make some people uncomfortable, it works to your advantage. Because we can argue either side of a case, we have a pretty good idea how the opposition will behave, and thus can prepare the proper defense and/or counterattack. This is why, in the world of criminal law, former state and federal prosecutors make the best defense attorneys. They know how the other side thinks.

And it's not just us lawyers who regularly switch sides. So do our expert witnesses. It's not uncommon for me to call a forensic accountant to testify for a client in the morning, and that same afternoon cross-examine that same forensic accountant when she testifies for the opposition in another case. When she testifies for me, she's an unassailable expert with unimpeachable credentials. But when she testifies for the other side, she's a hack-for-hire whose testimony can't be trusted.

That's just how the game is played.

You're the Boss

When you hire me as your legal counsel, that's just what you get: An advisor. A guide. A *consigliere*. I am effectively your employee. And that makes you the *boss*. My job is to devise legal strategies and tactics, but the ultimate decision(s) lies with you. And that includes accepting or rejecting settlement offers. All I can do is give you advice. The rest is up to you.

But beware. As the folks behind Marvel Comics' *Spider-Man* franchise are so fond of reminding us, "With great power comes great responsibility." You must accept ultimate culpability for the decisions you make.

If this makes you nervous, it should. Chances are, you've never gone through a divorce before. You don't really know what to expect or how to distinguish a good deal from a bad one.

Which is why you're hiring me. I have literally decades of experience playing this game. I know all the rules. I also know all the tricks. I have spent thousands of hours building relationships with other divorce attorneys and the judges before whom we argue. I know what's possible and what's not.

If I tell you you're getting the best possible deal, please believe me. You are. It doesn't matter what a friend says or what you may have read on the internet. I'm a professional, and I'm giving it to you straight. If that's not good enough, I'd advise you to fire me and look for a yes-man lawyer. I'll follow-up by sending you a CYA letter explaining that I gave you my best legal advice, which you rejected.

Which is your prerogative. Because you're the boss.

The Case of the Stubborn Stoner

Cameron and Claire were married with two kids, ages six and eight. Cameron was an up-and-coming musician. Claire had a stable job as an HR executive. After ten years, the ups and downs of Cameron's music career proved too much for Claire, and they agreed to divorce.

Cameron loved his kids and wanted full-time custody, claiming Claire was a workaholic who didn't have time to spend with their girls. Claire, on the other hand, accused Cameron of abusing drugs, particularly opiates. As Cameron's attorney, I advised him in no uncertain terms to stay clean. (Family law judges have little sympathy for stoners.)

One day, I received notice that Claire's lawyers had called an emergency custody hearing for that very afternoon. I ran to the courthouse in downtown Santa Ana and met Cameron in the lobby. It took me no time at all to see my client was high as Everest.

Luckily, opposing counsel had not yet arrived. I immediately dragged Cameron to a nearby coffee shop where I ordered him a double espresso and tried to talk him out of appearing that day.

"You don't look well," I said as politely as possible. "You need to go home. You can't be in court based on the way you look and how you're acting."

"I'm gonna do this," Cameron said, slurring his words. "I'm fine. I havta keep my girls."

"I'm advising you against this," I stressed.

"I told you. *I'm fine!*" he shouted, his eyes swimming.

I knew the court would take one look at Cameron and see he was on drugs, killing any reputable perception we had built. I even wrote him a letter (which I said he could read later when he was not high), that I emailed to him on the spot, explaining how this decision would cost him custody.

Still, at Cameron's insistence, we went to court. As predicted, it took the judge all of one second to recognize Cameron's inebriated state. He granted full custodial rights to Claire.

"How could you let me do that!?" he later demanded.

What could I say? I did everything I could to get the best results for him, but in the end, he made the unfortunate decision that hurt him.

You're Also Renting a Reputation

So far, we've talked about key factors that can determine an attorney's value, including education, experience, track record, and relationships with other lawyers. But there's one more important quality you're buying—or, more accurately, *renting*—when you hire an attorney, and that's your lawyer's reputation among judges.

Judges are, for better or worse, human beings, just like everyone else. They have their moods. They have their temperaments. And they have their biases. Although judges are supposed to be impartial umpires who are just there to call balls and strikes, as we often hear in Supreme Court confirmation hearings, they can't help but develop affinities for, or a dislike of, lawyers who appear before them regularly.

An attorney who has a reputation among judges for being professional, thorough, well-prepared, and effective in court is likely to benefit you more than one whom judges regard skeptically—or one who has no reputation at all. The ratings services cited previously can give you some indication of a prospective attorney's standing. Another source is the California State Bar Association, which holds records of any disciplinary actions that have been taken against members. Be sure to consider this when making your selection.

TEN WARNING SIGNS YOU HAVE A BAD LAWYER

1. They don't return your calls.

2. They don't file documents on time.

3. They don't show up to court.

4. They don't advise you well.

5. They don't listen.

6. They act condescending.

7. They don't protect you (from yourself).

8. They don't copy you on every document/letter/filing sent.

9. They represent you poorly to the court.

10. They are unprepared in hearings.

Divorce Isn't a DIY Project

Nearly five hundred years ago, the English poet Alexander Pope warned us, "A little learning is a dangerous thing."[1] What was true in the seventeenth century is even more so here in the twenty-first. Thanks to the internet, everyone is suddenly an expert. At least everyone *thinks* they are. And that's how they get into trouble.

For the last twenty years, the bane of every doctor's existence has been WebMD and similar medical self-help sites. Patients inevitably arrive at their offices with diagnoses already in hand along with an AI-generated course of treatment. And nine times out of ten, they're wrong. But try talking down someone convinced their joint pain is due to chikungunya fever because their symptoms match what they "read on the internet," when what they really have is common rheumatoid arthritis.

The same goes for divorce law. I can't tell you how many clients hire me for my expertise and then proceed to tell me how to handle their case because they "Googled it." (I dread what's going to happen when everyone starts using ChatGPT for this.)

For example, I had one client who insisted he should get half of the $500,000 equity bump on her $6 million separate property house that enjoyed an increase in value after their separation. When I asked him why he believed he was entitled to this, he said he had "looked it up on the internet."

When I told him he was wrong, he resisted strongly. So we retraced his steps and discovered he had found a site that discussed divorce law in *Florida*, a state whose rules are, in many respects like *this* one, different than those in California. Then there was the client who thought he could save money by writing my briefs for me. He believed he could simply download the appropriate templates, fill in the blanks, and trim some hours off my bill.

What he didn't understand was that I am legally and ethically obligated to create these documents myself so I can assure their accuracy. When clients take it upon themselves to do what should be *my* work, it just adds more hours to my day as I must review, double-check, and, as necessary, modify what they've done—which ends up costing them *more*. (In this case, that includes the additional hour I had to take explaining all this to my client.)

It's much simpler and cheaper to let me draft everything from the beginning. In short, you've hired me for a reason. Please let me do my job.

Changing Attorneys Midstream Is a Bad Idea— or Why I Won't Be the Third Lawyer

I'm sure it's no surprise to you that it's better to hire the right lawyer at the beginning of the divorce process than it is to hire and fire lawyers until you get it right. Just as in the marriage from which you're trying to extricate yourself, it's easier and cheaper, as well as more efficient and cost effective, to get it right the first time than it is to invest your energy, time, money, attention, and trust in someone, only to realize it's not working out.

Also, because laying out a compelling argument is my profession, I spell out in the following sections the reasons why switching lawyers in the middle of a case tends to be a *really* bad idea.

It wastes money. When you fire one attorney then hire another, the new lawyer needs to be brought up to speed. This takes time. And time is money. Also, the new lawyer may have a whole new approach to your case. This may mean making new motions, taking new depositions, filling new papers, and so on. All of which comes at an additional expense. Unfortunately, family law expenses aren't tax deductible. The money you spent on Lawyer #1 is money down the drain.

It makes you look bad in court. People who play musical chairs with their lawyers are generally looked at as flakes. Judges find them annoying. And do you really want to irritate your judge?

It undercuts your credibility. Getting a favorable divorce settlement often involves projecting an image of honesty, dependability, and stability. This is especially true when child custody issues are at stake. Replacing a legal team during a case projects just the opposite image. It makes you looks shifty, dishonest, unsure, and untrustworthy. In court, this is not a good look.

It hardens the opposition. Switching attorneys mid-case signals to the other side that you're in trouble. They see it as a sign of weakness and will usually respond by hardening their positions. This only puts you in a weaker position when negotiating.

It prolongs the suffering. Changing out your legal representation inevitably slows the process, costing not only money but emotional capital. The longer your divorce lasts, the more pain you are destined to endure. Like an invasive medical exam, a divorce is something you want to complete as fast as possible.

Good lawyers don't fire good clients, and good clients don't fire good lawyers.

The Case of the Demanding Diva

Max was a thirty-eight-year-old automobile products entrepreneur who had already gone through two divorce lawyers before a mutual friend referred him to me. As a favor to our friend, I agreed to consider Max's case. Reviewing his files, I saw that his first two lawyers had been excellent attorneys. I had gone up against both in court multiple times and knew they weren't pushovers.

As I was now going to be the third—and probably not the last—lawyer to go through Max's revolving door, I asked him point blank why he had fired his previous attorneys.

"They let me down."

"How exactly?"

"They didn't get the right information in my wife's deposition," Max replied. "She doctored my books. Took money from me. They couldn't get her to admit that."

"How do you know she did those things?"

"Because I *know*," Max insisted. "The money was missing. And that's just the kind of thing she'd do."

"Anything else?"

"Lots of things. Like, they didn't prep me for my own deposition."

"They didn't prep you at all?" This just didn't sound credible to me.

"Well, yeah, we had a few rehearsals, but still I ended up saying things I shouldn't have. They should have prevented that."

At this point, I didn't have to ask Max to continue. He was so wound up, there was no way to stop him even if I had wanted to.

"I gave them a whole bunch of suggestions, a whole list of questions to ask my wife, and they barely listened to me at all," he growled. "They did a horrible job questioning her, getting her to admit she's an unfit parent, which she obviously *is*. The last guy even charged me $25,000, and what have I got to show for it? *Nothing!*"

My instincts were right. Max was poison. I politely passed on his case.

Several months later, I learned Max had found another lawyer, fired *her*, and then finally settled on a fifth and final attorney. Not surprisingly, his settlement details were not particularly advantageous, even though his now-ex-wife made considerably more than he did.

Of note is that the judge failed to award him any needs-based fees to cover his expenses, something courts usually do under these circumstances, noting he had caused his own financial distress by arbitrarily hiring and firing his counsel. The bulk of his expenses had been spent on simply getting each new attorney up to speed rather than on the customary "expeditious prosecution" of his case.

Oh, and the last attorney? Max stiffed him and he had to take Max to court to collect his fees.

I really dodged a bullet with that one.

Why You Don't Want a Yes-Man

Max, the client described in the preceding narrative, is a classic case of someone shopping for a yes-man (or yes-woman) attorney. They're not seeking legal counsel. They're looking for an echo chamber. An employee to whom they can bark orders and who will blithely do their bidding.

I liken such people to "doctor shoppers" who go from one physician to the next until they find one who will tell them what they want to hear. You're thirty pounds overweight? No problem. You drink half a bottle of scotch a day? Not worried. You want more pain pills? Here, knock yourself out!

This is decidedly *not* what you want in a legal counsel. What you want is someone who *will* challenge you at every turn—because that's exactly what opposing counsel will do when they get the chance. You also want someone who can recognize what's actually best for you, which is not always the thing you think you want. You want someone who is not only smart but *wise*.

So you've hired your legal counsel. Congratulations! You've taken your first step toward emancipation. Now things are about to get real.

At this point, you're likely champing at the bit, eager to slice the Gordian knot that is your marriage as quickly and cleanly as possible. But, before we charge onto the playing field, we first must get our heads into the game. We must figure out exactly what "winning" will look like, as well as how we're going to get there.

This is not as easy as you may think.

5

PLAYING TO WIN, PART I

While a marriage is based on consensus, divorce is predicated on *conflict*. In a marriage, two people, whether motivated by love, obligation, pragmatism, or simple convenience, agree to form a partnership, an arrangement rooted in cooperation and compromise. Any marriage counselor will tell you that the longest-lasting marriages are those in which each participant recognizes, respects, and tries to satisfy the needs of the other.

Such (loving) accommodation involves everything from where to live, how money will be handled, how household chores will be divided, how many kids to have (if any), how the kids (if any) will be raised/disciplined, to where to vacation, what to have for dinner, what to watch on TV, at whose parents they will spend the holidays, and so on. Obviously, no marriage is without its points of friction ("spats," we sometimes like to call them). But these are usually resolved quickly with an apology, and the couple can get on with the business of enjoying each other.

Conversely, when couples divorce, self-interest becomes priority one. The give-and-take so essential to marriage devolves into a question of "take." No one wants to come out of a divorce feeling like the loser or that they've been taken advantage of. In this sense, divorces can resemble inheritance fights among previously congenial siblings when money and property is suddenly up for grabs. It's all roses and rainbows until young sister Patti makes a grab for the ruby necklace older sister Charlotte believes Mumsie promised to *her*.

That's when the claws come out.

You may hope for an amicable divorce in which you and your spouse calmly agree to part ways, dispassionately divide your assets, expeditiously arrive at a mutually amenable child custody arrangement, and then jauntily move on to your new lives, but, trust me, such divorces are the exception, not the rule. Most divorcing couples more closely resemble sweaty cage match fighters than they do the urbane sophisticates of some Noel Coward play. And in such circumstances, the only objective is to *win*.

The question then becomes, what does winning mean to *you*? What does winning *look like*? To you, winning may mean getting the house. Or it may be foisting that leaky old white elephant onto your ex and walking away with a fistload of cash. It may mean being awarded primary custody of your wonderful kids. Or it may mean leaving your ex to deal with those snot-nosed brats while you jet off with your new-found love to Cancun. It may mean seeing your ex is able to live in the style to which he or she has grown accustomed. Or it may mean leaving your ex destitute—or as close to it as you can manage.

It may mean a fresh new start. Or it may mean getting *revenge*.

Whatever your definition of winning is, it's best that you describe it to your attorney, *in detail*. This is important for three reasons:

- Your lawyer needs to know what you want so they can develop a plan to achieve it. As your attorney, they are obligated to act in your best interests. But if they don't know what you want, they can't deliver it.

- *You* need to know if your goals can be achieved or if you're just setting yourself up for disappointment. What you *want* to achieve and what you *can* achieve are often two wholly different things. Courts are particularly notorious for defying one's expectations. (More than one judge has exclaimed after stating their ruling, "I see both of you seem unhappy. That probably means I did my job." What they really mean is that if you want to leave all the decisions up to someone in a black robe who does not know you at all, they will gladly do so. You just may not like the result.)

- Together, you and your attorney must determine if your conditions for victory really are in your long-term best interests. Generally, people have a hard time separating *wants* from *needs*. This is particularly true when we're swept up in the tsunami of passions associated with any major life change, of which marital dissolution is one of the most profound. This is why having an objective, disinterested advisor, like an experienced family law attorney looking out for you is so critical to your long-term happiness.

As an attorney, it's my job to act pragmatically so I can move you as close as possible to your goals without jeopardizing your well-being or forcing you to needlessly spend too much time and/or money. The best divorce is generally a *quick divorce* in which you and your ex emerge emotionally whole and ready to move confidently into the next phase of your life.

Sixty-nine percent of divorces are initiated by the wife.[1]

Is It Worth It?

In the marketing industry, copywriters are taught to help customers distinguish between *cost* and *value*. Cost is what you pay for something. It's a specific, quantifiable amount. It's the number of dollars you pull from your wallet, the figure that appears on your monthly credit card statement.

Value, on the other hand, is what you get *out* of something. Perhaps this can be measured objectively, but just as often, value is purely subjective. It can be nothing more than an emotional response. A feeling. A sense of fulfillment.

For example, a Timex watch runs between $40 and $100. At the other end of the spectrum, a new Rolex will set you back between $7,000 and $50,000. Which is the better value?

Both keep accurate time. Yet wearing a Rolex imbues you with a level of status (among some people) no Timex can even attempt. Someone to whom status is not important probably couldn't imagine shelling out $7,000 for even a low-end Rolex, while someone who appreciates Rolex likely wouldn't be caught dead wearing a $100 Timex.

This is basic stuff. But now let's imagine you're offered a watch for $500. Is that a good deal or a bad one? Obviously, it depends on the watch. If it's a Timex, the offer is laughable. But if it's a genuine, mint condition Rolex, even the lifelong Timex buyer might jump at the opportunity. Because, for a genuine Rolex, $500 is an incredible *value*.

Or let's take the example of home improvement. When considering any major domestic remodeling project, real estate specialists will advise you to consider how much of the cost will actually add to the value of home at resale. The recovery percentage—or return on investment (ROI)—can vary wildly. For example, replacing a battered garage door with a new one has an average recovery value of nearly 100 percent. At the other end of the spectrum, a high-end master bedroom addition has an average ROI of less than 50 percent. And painting walls an unpopular color can add nothing or even *decrease* a home's resale potential.

I try to get my clients thinking the same way about their divorce, specifically how much they're likely to pay versus what they're actually going to get out of it. Some high-end divorces can cost hundreds of thousands of dollars (or more) to litigate. Is it worth it? Probably not if the assets at stake are just $500,000. But if we're talking about a $10–$150 million estate? Now the same *cost* starts to make sense. Heck, in such a case, $1 million may even be as much a bargain as our new garage door or hypothetical $500 Rolex watch.

When planning for your divorce, it's crucial to do a cost-benefit analysis of the expected outcomes. Accordingly, to get my clients the best possible *net* monetary settlement means assessing the costs in money, time, and brain damage of continuing litigation instead of accepting a reasonable settlement.

JOBS WITH THE HIGHEST DIVORCE RATES

Gaming (casino) managers: 52.9%

Bartenders: 52.7%

Flight attendants: 50.5%

Gaming (casino) services workers: 50.3%

Metal and plastic industrial workers: 50.1%[2]

"I Don't Care What It Costs!"

When I first meet with clients, they will often tell me that price is not an object.

"I don't care what it costs! I want that bitch/bastard destroyed!" they declare.

I tell them they're not being truthful with themselves.

"You say that now, but when the bill comes in, you'll care," I assure them. "When I hand you a bill for $100,000, or $50,000, or even $20,000 you'll care. Trust me. So let's find a way to make that bill as small as possible."

This piece of legal advice alone is worth the price of admission.

In Delaware, it's legal to file for an annulment if a friend dared you to marry your spouse.

The Case of the Vindictive Vapers

Let's call this client Kenny. Like the late country singer Kenny Rogers, Kenny had a round moon-face set off by a handsome gray beard. Unlike the late Mr. Rogers, as immortalized in his signature 1978 pop hit "The Gambler," our Kenny did not know when to hold 'em or when to fold 'em. He only knew how to go all in. Which did not serve him well in the long run.

Kenny owned a chain a vape shops. His wife, Barbara (Ken and Barbie. Cute, I know.) owned a chain of CBD dispensaries. Each was quite successful. Now, in their eighth year of marriage, each hated the other with white-hot passion. Each accused the other of hiding money in their businesses and of breaching their fiduciary responsibility to each other.

Both paid experts to embark on deep-dive discovery missions that made federal RICO investigations look cursory by comparison. They fought their own War of the Roses (the 1989 movie, not the fifteenth-century British dynastic imbroglio) as they made it their life's mission to make existence as painful as possible for the other.

When I entered the case on Kenny's behalf, the divorce was already in its third year. In the legal crossfire, both businesses had sustained lethal wounds and had folded, leaving several million dollars to be split between them. I advised Kenny to settle quickly to preserve what capital remained, but he'd hear none of it. It seemed as if the man would gladly burn through what few assets were left and accept a life of penniless destitution if it meant he could leave Barbara broke as well. Which is nearly what happened.

Because of the expenses incurred in the prolonged divorce, what had been businesses with a combined value in the tens of millions of dollars was, when the dust finally settled, worth just $1.5 million. In the end, the two walked away with about 750 grand, and no business to fall back on.

For this gambler, his all-in strategy was a bust.

Considering Child Custody

Any fan of Hollywood gangster films and TV shows knows that mob life, especially in the Italian Mafia, is governed by a strict set of unwritten rules. These include the following:

- Never seek justice from legal authorities (the *omertá*).

- All introductions must be made by a mutually known and trusted third party.

- Never be seen with cops.

- Respect wives (and never look at another man's).

- Don't involve civilians in gang wars.

This last rule is relevant to our discussion. In a divorce, your kids are the civilians. And you must do everything possible not to get them involved in your beef. Your divorce cannot be *their* divorce. You cannot use your kids as hostages, as human shields, or as leverage.

Don't ask your kids to choose sides. Don't subject them to depositions or ask them to testify in court. Don't ask them to spy on your ex. Don't use child custody details as bargaining chips. And please don't ever blame your problems on *them*.

The Case of the Appalling Parents

I'm going to warn you up front: this story has a tragic ending. I include it to illustrate the potentially high cost of involving children, no matter what their age, in their parents' divorce.

Israel and Caterina had one child, a son, named Amory. When Israel and Caterina began their divorce proceedings, Amory was fourteen years old, no longer a child but certainly not yet an adult.

From the case's onset, the couple violated virtually every rule concerning children. For starters, they demanded Amory choose which parent to live with. At first, Amory demurred. He didn't want to have to choose between his mother and his father. But then the couple hired Amory an attorney of his own, and the lawyer said he *had* to choose.

So Amory picked his dad. Israel was thrilled. Caterina, understandably, was not. In the following months, she retaliated by making Amory feel guilty about his choice. She then exploited this guilt by having him spy on his father, chronicling every parental indiscretion he could identify in a private journal.

Israel, for his part, fell right into Caterina's trap. To make Amory feel better about the choice he had made, Israel invited him out to party with the younger women he was now dating. This included partaking of alcohol and, later, drugs. By the time he was sixteen, Amory had become addicted to cocaine. Predictably, his schoolwork suffered tremendously, as did his social life and mental health.

As Amory went back and forth between parents, each tried to poison his mind against the other. Finally, between the anger, manipulation, and the drugs, Amory snapped.

On the very day Israel and Caterina were to go to court to finalize their divorce, Caterina arrived at her husband's condo to find the building surrounded by police cruisers. Much to her horror, she learned Amory had, just minutes earlier, jumped from the building's roof and killed himself.

Why I Sometimes Need to Be Aggressive

As a family law litigator, I can't be an a**hole all the time. But sometimes I do have to be one. Sometimes I have to be less than kind. Sometimes I have to be (or at least appear to be) unmovable. Sometimes I have to be loud and brash and even insulting. This is not my default way of interacting with others. But I can assume it as a tactic when required.

Personally, I *like* going to court. I like bare knuckles, hand-to-hand combat. (If only metaphorically.) But that doesn't mean this is always best for the client. There are occasions when diplomacy is much more effective than fisticuffs. There are times when seduction is more powerful than brute force. And there are situations when the mere *threat* of devastating pain is more potent than the actual administration of said savagery.

Two millennia ago, the Romans had a saying: "Si vis pacem, para bellum." It translates as, "If you want peace, prepare for war." This is how I get ready for court. I prepare for total war. I let the opposition know I'm doing so. And just as America's nuclear arsenal has served as an effective deterrent since the end of World War II, my promise of mutually assured destruction more often than not spurs the other side to seek a quick and minimally painless resolution.

Not only does this preparation help resolve more cases outside of court, but it is much less expensive than the alternative.

Today, 15 percent of adult women in the United States are either divorced or separated, compared with less than 1 percent in 1920.[3]

The One Where I Release My Inner A**hole

In trial law, a guiding principle advises us: never ask a question to which you don't already know the answer. A lawyer never wants to be surprised by a witness's response. Therefore, any attorney who feigns ignorance is likely leading said witness into a trap.

Which just happens to be one of my signature moves.

Jack (fifty-one) had filed for divorce against Brenda (forty-five) after fourteen years of marriage. This was the second marriage and second divorce for each. The couple had two sons, ages ten and eight, who had become the focus of a rather contentious child custody dispute. Brenda also had another daughter, Stephanie, now nineteen, from her previous marriage.

During the litigation, Stephanie called my office and volunteered to testify against her mom, whom she viewed as an unfit mother. She gave me two full pages of insults, rants, and other abusive behavior she had endured as a child. Describing Brenda as a dysfunctional alcoholic, Stephanie said she would even be willing to testify against her mother in court if it became necessary.

Now, I have already discussed my rule against involving children in a divorce. But this was different. Stephanie was the product of a previous marriage and so was not part of *this* divorce. Also, she was, at age nineteen, a grown woman of legal age, not a child, one who had come to *me* with an offer to testify. So my prohibition did not apply.

The day came for Brenda to testify. Prompted by her lawyer, she told the court about what she described as Jack's abusive behavior. She claimed Jack swore at her, belittled her, and humiliated her, all in front of their children. This, she insisted, made Jack an unfit parent and was cause for her to receive full custody of their sons.

Following Brenda's testimony, it was time for my cross-examination. I took a deep breath to center myself before reveling in what was about to be a great Perry Mason–esque moment. Then I prepared to unleash my inner a**hole. (What follows is a transcript of the proceedings—with certain identifying details changed.)

Paul: I have read your declaration, and you're asserting that Jack is abusive.

Brenda: Yes.

Paul: And this abuse is causing you a tremendous amount of psychological pain and hurting the kids, correct?

Brenda: Absolutely.

Paul: You are asserting he's calling you names like "b**ch" and "a**hole," telling you to "f**k off."

Brenda: Absolutely.

Paul: And how did that make you feel when he said that?

Brenda: It scared me and the kids.

Paul: Now, Brenda, *you* don't talk like that, do you? That's why you were so offended and scared by these words, right?

Brenda: I absolutely do not ever talk like that.

Paul: So you would never talk like that to your spouse, would you?

Brenda: No.

Paul: You would never talk like that to your friends, would you?

Brenda: No.

Paul: You would never talk like that to *anyone*, right? You don't speak like that at all?

Brenda: Absolutely not.

Paul: Especially, you wouldn't speak like that to your children, would you?

Brenda: Absolutely not. Never.

At that point, I approached her with Stephanie's text record of an actual exchange between Brenda and her. The two-page diatribe is astonishing in its malice. Here's just one highlight of some of the vilest things a mother could ever say to her daughter: "I can't believe you came out of my p****. I wish you were never born."

It put Alec Baldwin to shame.

I handed her Stephanie's affidavit. "Stunned" does not even begin to describe the look on her now pale face. Then I gave a copy to the judge.

Brenda: I can explain this—

Paul: Objection, Your Honor. No question pending. The witness has not been asked a question. Move to strike.

Judge: Sustained, it is stricken.

(In court, a witness cannot simply *volunteer* testimony. They can only respond to questions posed by either counsel or the judge.) So the judge properly sustained my objection, and her statement was stricken from the record. I now proceeded to ask Brenda authentication questions.

Paul: Is this a text message you sent?

Brenda: Yes, I sent it, but—

I cut her off with another objection, leaving only "Yes, I sent it" in the official court record, thereby authenticating it. I then read the text diatribe, word for word, before the judge stopped me halfway through the second page.

Judge: Mr. Nelson, I think we all get the idea here. Would you like to have that admitted into evidence?

Paul: Yes, I would, Your Honor.

It was admitted. I sat down. No further questions. Mic drop. I had set a trap, and the witness walked right into it.

If you are a smoker married to a nonsmoker, you are 75 to 91 percent more likely to get divorced than if both you and your spouse are smokers.[4]

Create a Checklist

When preparing for a divorce, create a checklist of everything you want to get in your settlement. Be as specific as possible. This way, your attorney can develop a comprehensive strategy for negotiations and, if necessary, help you modify your goals. Items to consider for your list include the following.

The house. If purchased during the marriage the house is presumed to be "community property," and each spouse is entitled to an equal share of it. There are exceptions, of course. For example, a house purchased prior to the marriage is considered the "separate property" of that spouse. Often, this item has strong nostalgic qualities for both parties. For this reason, especially, this asset can be a strong bargaining chip.

Investments. Unlike the family house, this is usually straight forward. The cash value of any jointly held stocks, bonds, 401(k)s, and other investments is determined at the time of final judgment and then divided equally among the spouses. The only exceptions here are holdings that can be deemed "separate property," which goes to the owner of that separate property, as discussed in an earlier chapter. (This is where the burden of tracing the funds falls on the person who claims it is separate.)

Debt. Just like assets, with rare exception, the court must equally divide debt as well.

- Credit card debt

- Vehicle loans

- Student loans

- Life insurance policies

- Long-term care insurance

- Private school tuition

- Outstanding lawsuits, including bankruptcies

- Net operating losses that are carried over to future tax years

Child custody arrangements. When minor children are involved in a divorce, the cliché is that primary custody goes to the mother and the dad gets them perhaps every other weekend. While such one-sided arrangements may have been common in decades past, modern custody arrangements tend to be much different (at least in California). Under California law, no parent can receive automatic preference. The court begins by considering the parents as equals. And unless you can provide evidence that your spouse is somehow unfit to assume equal custody—say, because of alcohol or drug dependency, a history of abusive behavior, or a job that keeps them away from home for extended periods—the court will most likely continue to see it that way.

When making its custody ruling, the court will prioritize the "children's best interest." So, if you want to make a case one way or the other, you must do so by arguing in terms of what is best for the children, not what is best for *you.*

Also, co-parenting is very important to the court but more important to your children. (The courts expect parents to work together for the best interest of their children, and shared custody is one such way to accomplish this.) Shared custody can be accomplished by following one of several possible arrangements:

- Each parent gets custody every other week. (A common approach with older children.)

- 2-5-2: Two days with one parent, five days with the other. Example: every Monday and Tuesday with Mom, and then Wednesday and Thursday with Dad while alternating each weekend. (On alternate weeks, each parent has a five-day stint with the children.) This is probably the most common equal sharing schedule. The result: the children don't go five days without seeing the other parent.

- Who gets the kids on holidays, vacations, birthdays, and other special occasions? Generally, parties equally share these times and alternate them every other year.

- Finally, how are finances associated with coming-of-age events like communions, baptisms, bar/bat mitzvahs, quinceañeras, proms, graduation parties, and the like to be handled? Will they be split down the middle? As a function of each parent's annual gross income? Some other formula? Your preferred solutions should all be part of your checklist. Some of these points will not be addressed by the judge. It is up to you and your ex to figure it out.

Documentation. Speaking of kids, who holds on to their key documentation like birth certificates, passports, medical and immunization records, and so on? If one ex-spouse dies, how will the survivor be able to access these documents? This is an issue often overlooked in early divorce discussions.

Jewelry. Any gifted jewelry such as rings, watches, necklaces, bracelets, and the like usually become separate property and remain the property of the person it was gifted to. Yes, this even includes wedding and engagement rings. Exceptions exist, but this is the norm.

In Kentucky, you are not allowed to divorce and remarry more than four times.

Why "I Want to Destroy My Ex" Is a Warning Sign

Telling your lawyer you want to destroy your ex in your divorce is a big fat red flag. It signifies you want to do harm. Which is not what family court is designed for. Family court operates differently from other parts of the law. When practicing family law, an attorney can be sanctioned by the court for prolonging a case. When you go on a tear about destroying the other party (via your attorney) that doesn't bode well. Yes, of course, zealous advocacy is okay. But it's best to temper expectations.

The Case of the Vindictive Daddy

This is another story of an out-of-control divorce with tragic consequences. Be warned.

Tim and Sara were married for eleven years. They had two young daughters, ages eight and six. Gina was unhappy with Tim and began an affair with Tim's ex-business partner, Steve. The affair went on for two years, at which point Tim discovered his wife was cheating on him.

He immediately filed for divorce.

Eighteen months later, the case was settled. Gina (my client) had, by now, moved in with Steve, so she and Tim were able to sell their four-bedroom house and evenly split the proceeds. They agreed on a co-parenting arrangement, with each getting custody of the girls every other week.

But a clean break with Gina was not enough for Tim. Still livid and vengeful at having been cuckolded, he decided he would use their daughters as pawns in what could only be described as a scorched-earth strategy. He knew that in California, a family law judgment is always subject to modification as circumstances change, and he devised to use this loophole in his favor.

On an almost monthly basis, Tim filed for changes concerning financial support and custody arrangement. He accused Steve of sexually mistreating the girls and called Child Protective Services (CPS) a whopping thirteen times, triggering multiple police investigations, which traumatized his daughters. To demonstrate that he was a "responsible parent," he found a job that paid substantially more than his previous employment and then remarried.

Through his legal machinations, Tim acquired primary custody, at which point he and his new wife moved forty miles away just so they could limit the amount of time Gina and Steve could spend with them. This forced the girls to change schools, which only added to their emotional turmoil.

When he had custody of his daughters, Tim wasted little time bad-mouthing their mother and characterizing Steve as some kind of sex fiend. This made the girls uneasy during the times they still spent with Gina—which was exactly Tim's intention.

Tim and his new wife eventually had a child of their own, and

Tim did what he could to blend his girls with his new family. Then COVID-19 hit, forcing the girls to stay home and cutting them off from their friends and social network. In response, the older daughter, now nearly a teenager, began self-cutting, a classic cry for help. But Tim, more interested in torturing Gina, didn't see the warning signs. Not until she ended up in the hospital for mental issues.

Again, children are not game pieces to be used in pursuit of some perceived victory over one's ex. When used for gain, it is *they* who pay the price.

Expectations Can Change

Chaos theory—the mathematical postulate made famous in Michael Crichton's 1990 sci-fi best-seller *Jurassic Park*—suggests the more elements a system has, the harder it is to know how those elements will behave over time, thus the harder it is to predict future outcomes. This is why things like the weather, the economy, and political campaigns are notoriously difficult to forecast. Even small deviations from established norms can, over time, have complex (and unforeseen) consequences. Also, the farther out in time you go, the harder forecasting becomes.

What's true for meteorology, economics, and political science also holds true for family law. Many elements go into a divorce, making final outcomes difficult to predict. And the longer a divorce drags on, the more surprises are likely to come your way. This is why I always advise clients to be ready to adjust expectations.

Victory is a moving target; the longer a divorce continues, the more one's initial expectations can change, especially as new information is revealed. Therefore, it makes sense to reevaluate your priorities as time goes on, assessing and reassessing what your goals are and the likelihood of achieving them based on evolving on-ground realities.

In this chapter, we look at some of the myriad factors you should consider when preparing for a divorce. If you've been following along, you have established your priorities, created your checklist, and have articulated your preferred outcomes. But this is just the first step. Now it's time to take this information and use it to create an actionable battle plan.

6

PLAYING TO WIN, PART II

I n the previous chapter, I pose the question: What does winning look like to *you*? This is critical because every person contemplating divorce has a very different, very personal concept of victory. Divorce isn't an athletic competition in which "winning" can be objectively assessed by means of tallying runs, how many times a leather ovoid is moved into the opposition's end zone, or the number of truncated icosahedrons kicked into an adversary's net. As we explored, it's not only the disposition of joint property in question but also the ex-spouses' relationships with their children and the nature of any ongoing relationship the ex-spouses have with each other.

In effect, the terms of one's divorce effectively define the shape of one's future. Which makes divorce literally *existential* in nature. With so much at stake, one needs an advocate who thinks not only strategically, like a seasoned general, but also prudently, like a trained scientist.

What does science have to do with divorce?

Well, both disciplines deal with *laws*. But with an obvious, fundamental difference. Civil and criminal law is a wholly human construct. It varies not only from nation to nation but also from state to state, even from year to year. What's legal in one county can be a crime just across the border. (Itself wholly imaginary.)

What was verboten one year can become perfectly acceptable the next. In some US states, there was a time when it was illegal to marry someone of a different race. (It was called miscegenation.) There was also a time when it was legal to own another human being. In 1919, the eighteenth Amendment made the sale of alcohol illegal in the United States. In 1933, the twenty-first Amendment made it legal again. And let's not even talk about changing marijuana laws . . .

By contrast, scientific laws are the fundamental, unalterable principles governing the behavior of the universe. They existed long before the first *Homo sapiens* stood upright on the African savannah, and they will endure long after our planet has been swallowed by the bloated remnants of our dying sun.

The law of thermodynamics was created along with the universe itself. The speed of light is 186,282 miles everywhere in the Milky Way as well as in all the hundreds of millions of galaxies beyond. Scientific laws are things we *discover*, not things we *create*.

While written laws have been around since the time of Babylon's King Hammurabi (1792–1750 BC), what we now call the scientific method has only been around for about four centuries. It's based on observation and evidence-gathering. At the heart of the scientific method is the hypothesis, an educated guess that one puts to the test by rigid experimentation and repetition, removing as many variables as possible.

The hypothesis is also one of a divorce lawyer's most powerful tools.

For example, perhaps I have a client who states, "My husband and I bought our house for $1,700,000 using a $400,000 inheritance I received from my mother as a down payment. When we sell the house, I want that $400,000 back. It belongs to me."

That my client is owed $400,000 from her house sale is her hypothesis.

To prove or disprove her claim, I need evidence. By carefully examining the house's original sales documents, period bank records, and her mother's will, I can substantiate that my client did, in fact, use $400,000 in separate property to purchase the home in question for $1,700,000 two decades prior. Further, I can present such documentation *in court* in a way opposing counsel cannot dispute. If I can do this, she unquestionably is, under California law, entitled to $400,000 off the top of any sale.

But what if we don't have all the documents? Does that mean all hope is lost? Fortunately, no. There are other ways to prove things in court. Unlike in science, in court, an uncontroverted statement by a client is sufficient to establish a fact. *This is why credibility in court matters.* If you present well in court, the judge may side with you. Other methods like family expense method—essentially showing all community earnings went to pay for expenses, so anything else must have come from separate property—can also prevail.

But if a hypothesis is just flat out *wrong*—if I can't support it with evidence, uncontroverted testimony, or other accepted methods—I won't pursue it. That's only logical. And it happens to be how I practice law.

CALIFORNIA DIVORCE FACTS

- There are 1.2 million divorced men currently living in California.

- There are 1.7 million divorced women currently living in California.

continued

- California was the first no-fault state in America (1970).

- California law requires spouses to treat each other like business partners, each having a fiduciary responsibility to the other. This duty continues throughout a divorce case and ends only when a judgment is entered.

- California courts do not have power over a spouse who does not live in the state, was not served in the state, and has not lived in the state for at least six months.

- Once a divorce is filed, an automatic restraining order on both parties is put in place. Approximately 10 percent of divorced individuals violate this order.[1]

The Case of the Forthright Philanderer

Being credible in court can be crucial to winning a case. This is especially true when forensic evidence isn't available and first-person testimony is all the court has to consider.

Rudy was a successful insurance broker. When divorcing his wife of fifteen years, he claimed he had used $200,000 in separate property as the down payment on their Irvine, California, house, which now had a value of $1.2 million.

Unfortunately, Rudy was sloppy with his personal record-keeping and could not prove where the $200,000 had come from so many years earlier. His bank, which erased its financial records after seven years, was of no help.

Fortunately, Rudy was refreshingly honest—some might even say brutally so—in court. For example, opposing counsel noted Rudy withdrew $25,000 from the couple's joint bank account just weeks before filing for divorce.

The judge asked Rudy what the money was for.

"Surgery," Rudy replied without hesitation.

"What kind of surgery?" the judge asked.

"Breast enhancement."

This struck the judge as odd. "I assume *not* for yourself?"

"That is correct—it was for Lisa."

"And who is Lisa?" the judge pressed.

"My girlfriend," Rudy said with the barest of shrugs.

Although it was not his finest hour, Rudy had shown he was prepared to be honest, even when it made him look bad. Which, ironically, made him look *good* to the court. So, when it came time to rule on Rudy's separate property claim, the judge ruled in his favor based on his uncontroverted testimony, which was detailed and specific in time and amounts.

Like I said, in court, credibility is everything.

ORANGE COUNTY DIVORCE FACTS

- On average, thirty-three people file for divorce every day in Orange County.

- More than two thousand divorce attorneys currently practice there.

- Newport Beach has the highest divorce rate in the county.

- The divorce rate among members of the Orange County Fire Authority is 29 percent, more than double that of other area fire departments.[2]

The Case of the Nebulous Nuptials

In a memorable episode of the classic 1990s NBC comedy series *Friends*, Ross and Rachel drunkenly get married at the Chapel of Love in Las Vegas, Nevada. To further complicate matters, Ross then dupes Rachel into thinking they got the marriage annulled when they really didn't.

Sounds like a typical silly sitcom premise, right?

But sometimes, art imitates life. And vice versa. Roger and Belinda fell in love and, like so many couples, got married.

At least Belinda thought they had.

The "wedding," held in the backyard of Roger's three-thousand-square-foot hillside home with more than two dozen friends and relatives in attendance had looked real enough but had been simply ceremonial. Roger had never obtained a marriage license; nor had he submitted any other documentation to the county clerk.

The marriage was a sham.

Roger later admitted this was a kind of sick "insurance policy." If things didn't work out, he could say, "We were never really married" and thus avoid the hassle and expense of divorce. After all, California doesn't recognize common-law marriages.

So how'd that work out for Roger?

Actually, not so great. While they were "married," Roger and Belinda started a business. He contributed half; she kicked in the other 50 percent. Roger put the entire enterprise in his name. When Belinda questioned this, Roger explained that California being a community property state, she was automatically entitled to half their assets. Putting the business in his name just made paperwork simpler without threatening her financial stake.

Eight years later, the company was worth millions.

Roger figured this was the time to cash out, taking everything for himself. Belinda was dumbstruck. What about her half? This is when Roger dropped the bomb: they were never legally married. Psych!

But Belinda was no fool. She sued Roger and took him to court.

Roger's lawyer argued the law: Since the couple had never legally married, Belinda was only entitled to an amount equal to her initial investment, plus interest. As the business was solely in Roger's name, the remaining equity was his and his alone.

Belinda's attorney argued that Belinda had acted in good faith. She honestly believed she had married Roger and had put her faith in him. Roger, the attorney argued, had clearly acted in *bad* faith, committing fraud, and having done so, he should not be able to reap the rewards of his malfeasance.

Upon considering both arguments, the judge ruled in favor of Belinda. He awarded her half the business as a putative spouse, meaning that the marriage, although not technically legal, had been treated as if it had been. Moral of the story: what's funny in a sitcom can be deadly serious and expensive in real life.

Now, let's get into some winning strategies in part two of our discussion.

Winning Strategy 1: Put Them behind the Eight Ball

Most people spend more time planning their summer vacations than they do contemplating the possibility of divorce. But divorce is like an illness: the sooner you start dealing with it, the less long-term damage it's likely to wreak.

Let's switch metaphors here for a moment and liken divorce to one of its most popular analogs: warfare. What's one of the best ways to win a war? Start a year before the other side.

When war looks like a distinct possibility, a smart government will begin making necessary preparations. It will recruit and train troops. It will buy new equipment and make sure plenty of spare parts are available. Intelligence agencies will gather as much information as they can on the enemy's positions, strategies, and capabilities. Generals will devise a range of battle plans and wargame the likely scenarios.

Then, when war becomes inevitable, *strike first*.

This was exactly how Israel defeated the much larger combined armies of Egypt, Syria, and Jordan in the Six-Day War of June 1967. Conflict had been brewing in the Middle East since the previous November when attacks by Palestinian guerilla groups triggered Israeli reprisals in Jordan and Syria. Tensions escalated throughout the following spring until Egyptian president Gamal Nassar decided to show his support for Syria by using his navy to blockade Israel's southern port city of Eilat on the Gulf of Aqaba.

But Israel was ready.

It had been monitoring the activities of its Arab neighbors closely since the country's creation two decades earlier. It had already fought two wars with Egypt, the last in 1956, and had spent the previous twelve years building one of the most formidable militaries in the world. Its intelligence service, the Mossad, was second to none.

Early on the morning of June 5, 1967, Israel responded to the Egyptian blockade by launching a massive, well-coordinated air attack on its western neighbor. Within hours, Israel wiped out 90 percent of Egypt's air force while it was still on the tarmac.

Israeli tanks then swept through the Sinai all the way to the Suez Canal while at the same time, in the east, Israel responded to Jordanian shelling of East Jerusalem with another devasting armor assault. It was all over in six days. Israel now controlled the strategic Golan Heights, East Jerusalem, the West Bank of the Jordan River, the Gaza Strip, and the entire Sinai Peninsula. It was in the perfect position to negotiate a cease fire.

All because it had prepared for this fight *years* in advance.

If you're married, you should approach divorce the same way. Get ahead of things. Don't be reactive. If you're caught by surprise, you're likely to find you have no place to live, that key documents are unavailable or have suddenly "disappeared," and that events are happening far faster than your ability to handle them. Give yourself the head start you need to stake out an advantageous position.

This is exactly what I did with one of my earliest clients, Anthony. Anthony had a super-successful mail order business we estimated was worth $20 million. He claimed he funded the business fifteen years earlier with a mere $10,000 from his own savings. (He said his wife had not contributed any money of her own; nor had she participated in the business in any way.)

Although Anthony and his wife were, at this point, getting along just fine, I insisted Anthony document his entire business history ASAP to prove his sole ownership. It took him about six months to recover all the necessary records, but he was eventually successful. Which was a good thing, because in the final phase of this document discovery, he also discovered his wife was having an affair. (Ouch.)

So he was ready. When the time came to divorce and divvy up assets, we could prove beyond doubt that Anthony's business was entirely his own. Had Anthony not done this work in advance, the shock of his wife's infidelity—coupled with the emotional roller-coaster that followed—likely would have made it far harder and could have cost him literally millions of dollars.

In-Spouse and Out-Spouse

No trip to California is complete without a stop at one of our legendary In-N-Out burger restaurants. Founded in Baldwin Park in 1948, the family-owned chain now operates more than 350 restaurants throughout the west and southwestern United States, serving a menu limited to burgers, French fries, soft drinks, and shakes.

In addition to naming a great burger chain, "in-n-out" can be used to describe how the State of California recognizes and rewards divorcing spouses when a business is involved. Assuming the business is not a true fifty-fifty partnership, the spouse who *runs* the company is known as the "in-spouse." The one who is either uninvolved or serves in a minority role is the "out-spouse."

In a divorce, the court awards the in-spouse the business. This individual must pay the out-spouse half its value as part of any community property settlement. In other words, if you own and operate a business, you don't have to worry about the courts giving it to your spouse to run it into the ground; you will still have control.

You'll just have to pay for the privilege.

The Case of the Wicked In-Spouse

Again, in a divorce, there is a distinct benefit to being an in-spouse who is awarded an income-producing asset, such as a business. You can then use this income to pay spousal and/or child support and perhaps even pay off your ex's share over time rather than plunder your cash reserves or take out a loan to do so. But if you're the out-spouse in this scenario, the person who is being paid via the income your ex's property produces, be careful.

All may not be what it seems.

Playing to Win, Part II

Case in point: Amanda and Dallas owned a rental apartment building and several small retail locations. Amanda managed all the sites while Dallas pursued his dream of being a fine artist. When they divorced after eight years of marriage, Amanda, being the in-spouse, got Dallas to agree to a stipulated judgment, an agreement on property division, in which she would assume ownership of all encumbered real estate (property that was mortgaged) and Dallas would hold an IOU on the funds he was owed.

On the surface, this seemed reasonable. Instead of paying Dallas off right away, Amanda could focus on paying down her debt. Meanwhile Dallas maintained his claim on half of Amanda's equity, plus interest.

But Amanda was a crafty one. She never had any intention of paying Dallas a damned thing. Years before their divorce, she hid her income and profits in an elaborate web of shell corporations, LLCs, and dummy partnerships.

When Dallas came calling for the money he was owed, Amanda could open her books and plead poverty. Like Hollywood motion picture studios that curiously appear to lose money on every movie they make, Amanda appeared—on paper—to be going deeper into the red with every passing year.

Realizing something was rotten in the state of California, Dallas hired me to represent him. It took me literally years to untangle the web Amanda had weaved, and even then, we were unsure we had discovered every duplicity she had committed. Still, in the end, the money Dallas was forced to invest in me made the sizable gains he was able to claim well worth it.

Although I found Amanda thoroughly amoral (and I'm being kind here), I had to give her credit. She had studied her Sun-Tzu. She had prepared for war years in advance. And then she struck first.

Hopefully, Dallas learned his lesson and won't let anyone get the drop on him ever again. Talk about securing your interest in a division of community assets.

Winning Strategy 2: Make Them an Offer They Can't Refuse

In the popular mind, the divorce process climaxes with a trial where the spouses hash out their differences before a judge. But while *Kramer vs. Kramer*–style trials do occur, they can and *should* be avoided if possible.

The preemptive settlement helps accomplish this.

When a divorce is imminent, one of the litigants, usually the primary breadwinner, proposes an attractive settlement to incentivize the spouse to close the case and move on. (This is comparable to the defendant in a lawsuit making the plaintiff a large up-front offer to avoid further litigation and the associated costs.) For this strategy to work, the offer must be substantial and in line with the presumed value of the couple's holdings so as not to be offensive.

The keyword here is "presumed."

Take a client whom we'll call Dr. Drew. Dr. Drew cheated on his wife, whom we shall call Connie, for years. Consequently, Connie had every reason to hate her husband. And she did. With a vengeance.

Recognizing Dr. Drew was vulnerable, I advised him to avoid court and instead close the case with a preemptive offer. Dr. Drew agreed. The question was, how large should the offer be?

Step one was to determine the value of the doctor's estate. To do this, I hired a forensic accountant to look at the family's cash, property holdings, and business valuation from every angle. The advantage of using a forensic accountant is that her report is work product and is *not discoverable*. In other words, Connie's lawyers have no right to access this privileged information.

Ultimately, the forensic accountant determined that Dr. Drew's estate was likely worth between $20 million and $30 million. A full-blown forensic audit was not and could not be done in the time we had. But it was good enough to make a reasonable offer to try to end this before it had even begun. Under California's community property law, Connie was legally entitled to half his estate, as all of it had been acquired during their marriage.

But, just like Dr. Drew had been ignorant of his worth before the audit, Connie believed the value to be substantially less than our best estimate. In fact, Dr. Drew suspected she believed he was worth only a fraction of the actual total.

Dr. Drew made Connie a reasonable $10 million offer (based on the limited forensic work we had completed)—certainly enough to get her attention but possibly or even likely saving Dr. Drew millions. Just as eager to rid herself of him as he was to get away from her, Connie jumped at the offer, and the deal was done. Dr. Drew was thrilled. Not only had he avoided court, but he had possibly saved himself $5 million. (The $10 million he paid out turned out to be a fair result for both parties. Why? Dr. Drew took risks to achieve this outcome. For instance, if he had erred in the process, it could just as easily have blown up in his face. However, in this scenario, he came out ahead because of his preemptive due diligence.)

Forensic accountants are essential in high-value divorce cases. Yes, they're expensive, but the protected information they provide can be invaluable. Also, for the preemptive offer strategy to work, you must act first, you must be fast, and you must be fair. For Dr. Drew, his offer was based on the low number the forensic provided. It is certainly possible that he overpaid but more likely that he got a good solid deal—fair for both of them.

Had Connie taken the time to hire her own forensic accountant, she might have discovered their estate was worth more than she believed. However, again, the $10 million offer was so enticing—and more than fair based on her assumptions—that her desire for vengeance was satisfied.

In the end, that's what good divorce law is all about: closing a case quickly with both sides feeling they got a fair deal. In the end, the court will uphold an agreement where each party gets the benefit of the bargain.

THE FIVE REASONS YOU NEED TO PREPARE FOR YOUR DIVORCE—*NOW!*

Most banks destroy customer records after seven years. Likewise, many businesses have a similar designated document destruction policy, making the need for early identification critical.

Other documents can be tough to locate (e.g., credit card docs, corporate docs, marriage licenses, inheritance deposits, etc.) When divorce proceedings begin, record-hunting is *not* what you want to be thinking about.

Starting early allows you time to gather and build your case *before* the other side even knows there *is* another side.

We need to know what we don't know, such as the following:

- Is the prenup/postnup valid?

- Estate planning documents must be analyzed for a legal opinion; what is their upside and downside?

- Titles need to be pulled to assess legal ownership.
- Loan and escrow documents on the real property can gauge community and separate property division.
- Completing a diary on how much time you spend with your kids will build a stronger case demonstrating you *are* the primary parent.

Art of the (Divorce) Deal

Unlike criminal law, family law is not binary. In a criminal case, defendants are found either guilty or not guilty. It's one or the other. There is no halfway or in-between. Juries cannot rule "kinda."

But family law is different. Family law is all about compromise. This is especially true in California which, being a no-fault state, does not attempt to pin the blame for a marriage's failure on one party or the other, but instead tries to reach an accommodation that works for both parties.

There are good reasons for this.

For one, as stated earlier, California treats married couples as business partners with fiduciary responsibilities to each other. Also, in many instances, children are involved, and courts don't want to drag kids through a long, contentious fight.

This is what makes family law unique. In family court, you can actually be *ordered* to negotiate with the other side. (Although the court can't order you to agree.) This is actual law. It's in the statutes. Failure to be reasonable in litigation and attempts to settle can cost you dearly.

This dependence on negotiation is the main reason why divorces take so long to finalize. (Fifteen months, on average.) Every point of the agreement must be argued back and forth until an accommodation is reached. Still, when negotiating, we must be cautious about the following:

- Not responding to good-faith offers

- Responding with bad-faith offers

- Increasing the litigation's costs and time for no good reason—or a thin one

If you do any of these, you can be sanctioned (fined) by the court. It's called "frustrating the policy of the law," and it's covered in California Family Code 271.[3] So don't think you can win a favorable settlement just by digging in your heels!

In fact, as a family law attorney, one of my main jobs is to advise my clients when their insistence or resistance threatens to cross the line into obstruction. If it starts to look like they're being unreasonable or simply obstinate for its own sake, the court can strike back with a sanction. And that is something *nobody* wants.

When beginning negotiations, my strategy is always to settle the easy stuff first. This puts the opposition in an agreeable mood and shows the other side that we're negotiating in good faith. That we are being reasonable.

As we get deeper into the weeds, I identify those issues in which the opposition is adamant about and those for which they seem to have flexibility. Often, attorneys will label some item a must-have when they're really just creating a bargaining chip, something they can later sacrifice to obtain the prize they truly want. Learning to separate your opponent's must-haves from the nice-to-haves is essential for a successful negotiation.

Fortunately, in 75 to 80 percent of cases, we can settle *everything* in negotiations and never have to go to court. This makes everyone happy. The spouses. The lawyers. The court. The kids. We all get to shake hands and go on our merry ways.

But what happens when we encounter issues about which we can find *no* accommodation? *This* is when, and only when, we go to court.

Let's be clear, going to court is a last resort. Not only is it expensive, but there's always a chance, no matter how well one argues a case, that the judge will rule against you. That's the kind of unpredictability I always try to avoid.

Am I afraid of going to court?

Hell, no. I relish the opportunity. The courtroom is where I shine brightest. At the same time, I know that clients who go to court can often be surprised. One judge is deciding your future. Bystanders—meaning, kids—can be harmed too.

So, in this sense, I liken myself to a black belt karate master. I don't go looking for trouble. I try to settle conflicts peacefully whenever possible. But if I must attack, I do so swiftly and with brutal efficiency.

If you are an opposing attorney, don't give me a reason to don my gi (a lightweight garment worn in martial arts). You won't like me when I'm in my corner ready for battle.

Discovering Discovery

Before you go to trial, your attorney will conduct what we call *discovery*. Simply put, discovery is the pretrial phase during which each side exchanges information about the case at hand.

The idea behind discovery is that each side should be made fully aware of what evidence *might*—and I repeat, *might*—be presented at trial so everyone can prepare an adequate cross-examination, should the need arise. It was instituted by our court system to avoid "trial by ambush," in which one side would try to discredit the other by presenting evidence that catches it by surprise.

Discovery devices include the following.

Depositions. This is sworn out-of-court testimony. They are conducted in a traditional Q&A format, and the person being deposed must answer honestly or face possible perjury charges.

Interrogatories. These are written questions one side submits to the other, usually to clarify matters of fact. Interrogatories help establish the agreed-on details of the case and serve as foundation for an ensuing trial.

Requests for admissions. This is a set of statements one litigant sends to the other to be either confirmed or denied. Like the interrogatories, these help establish the parameters of the case under review.

Request for production of documents. In a divorce, this usually involves records concerning the couple's property holdings, investments, business records, and so on.

Subpoenas. Getting information from a third party like a credit card issuer or a bank.

Please note: In a divorce, you are automatically obligated to provide this information. (The courts require a full financial disclosure within sixty days of filing for divorce for both parties.)

Although discovery is supposed to prepare each side for trial, in practice, it usually helps *avoid* trial. This is because, once each side knows everything the other does, it becomes much easier to assess each side's relative strengths and weaknesses and thus determine the case's most likely outcome.

The Case of the Jerky Jeweler

Boris owned a successful wholesale jewelry business. Although he was able to bedeck his wife, Natalie, in enough necklaces, bracelets, and rings to satisfy a European duchess, the humiliation wrought by his habitual philandering ultimately tipped his wife's cost-benefit analysis toward divorce.

When the process began, I reached out to Boris's attorney, and we had a typical, congenial phone call during which I made the predictable request for his client's business records. The opposing attorney, having been down this road a gazillion times, said that would not be a problem.

(Morgan Freeman voice: "It *was* a problem.")

Thirty days later, I called the attorney again to report I had not received any documents. The attorney said I would need to put my request in writing. Which I did. I asked for his client's QuickBooks records for the past twenty-four months. I also requested a breakdown of his Charles Schwab brokerage account.

Another month passed without a response. So I called again. The attorney said I needed to make my requests *more* specific. At the same time, he made several accusations against my client, Natalie, blaming her for stealing from Boris.

By now alarm bells rang in my head. I had dealt with this family law attorney multiple times. He had never behaved this way.

"Boris is stalling, isn't he?" I said, more a statement than a question.

The attorney refused to confirm his client's culpability, but it was clear to me that Boris was just being a jerk. Worse, he was *enjoying* being a jerk.

My response was to file a motion with the court, charging Boris with a failure to comply with duly filed discovery requests.

Ultimately, the court agreed with me and fined him $50,000 for discovery abuses, including:

- Uncooperative behavior

- Unrealistic positions in trial not well-founded in law

- Making claims with no legal authority

Ultimately, there is no benefit to fighting a discovery request. When you try to hide things, it only makes the other side look harder.

Winning Strategy 3: When It *Does* Make Sense to Drag Things Out

I have repeatedly said the best divorces are *fast* divorces. The quicker you wrap things up, the less collateral damage you're likely to cause and the fewer chances there will be for things to go *horribly wrong*. (And, given enough time, things *will* go horribly wrong. It's a law of the universe.)

This advice is 100 percent consistent, unconditional, and irrevocable—95 percent of the time. In the other 5 percent, it kinda makes sense to drag things out.

Do you want the average two-year divorce, the five-year extended version, or the seven-year jumbo model? It all depends on your goals.

The Long Goodbye (Applying Strategy 3)

Amy and her brother, Nick, owned a successful San Diego–area construction business. Their specialty was large industrial buildings, the type used for factories, warehouses, and distribution centers. It was a high-stress, high-risk enterprise, the two having to constantly deal with material and labor issues, changing environmental regulations, and the cost of money. She and Nick often had to use their private assets as collateral to secure vital loans.

The high stress and long hours proved too much for Amy's husband, Derrick, and the two agreed to divorce. I represented Amy. Normally, I would have advised her to settle the matter as quickly and cleanly as possible. But Amy's specific goals convinced me to alter my methods to obtain Amy's best results.

As things stood, if the divorce was settled or tried in the usual two to two and a half years, Amy would have to give Derrick half her business value under California's community property laws. As the business was, on paper, worth millions, buying Derrick out was not something Amy wanted or was even able to do. Her company cash reserves were always low, and, as noted, most of her personal assets were being used as collateral against large business loans.

Amy ultimately decided she would be much better off—and happier—if she sold the business altogether or just let the business die a natural death. She made her money, and the risk of pledging all her assets for each new project was just not worth it anymore.

But still, this exiting process was going to take time. Years, even.

Which is why we stalled.

I pushed for extra time so that Amy could sell her business or otherwise make it go away and get out. Just prior to the divorce, she and her brother agreed to list their business construction warehouse as proof she was not doing more projects. She extricated herself from recurring revenue, and her brother decided not to sign any more guarantees of personal assets, thereby causing the natural death to her business she wanted anyway.

After five long years, Amy and her brother walked away from their business. Now, instead of having to give Derrick half the company, she only had to split the community assets, but no value was assigned to the business and no cash flow was assigned to her for purposes of support. In fact, we settled support for pennies on the dollar.

This strategy will not always work, but in this instance, I knew the odds of rolling the dice and we ended up taking full odds on a hard eight. Stalling the divorce saved Amy millions. It was an unusual resolution for an unusual situation, but it made sense.

In law, as in comedy, timing is everything.

WARNING SIGNS YOUR SPOUSE MAY BE PLANNING TO DIVORCE YOU

- Your man comes home smelling like someone else's perfume
- Your wife wants new boobs but has no sexual interest in you
- Your spouse has had a "headache" for a looong time
- Your spouse wants to move to a different state with no good explanation
- Your spouse suddenly needs access to documents like deeds, corporate documents, and access to the safety deposit box

A Word on Fiduciary Duty/Automatic Duty

During your divorce, your attorney should ask you for regular updates (and you should tell them of significant changes as well), every three to six months, regarding changes, if any, to your financial situation. Is business up or down? Are you in the mortgage banking business when interest rates hit a thirty-year high? Maybe it is time to try to settle your case or get it to trial ASAP. Did you lose your job? Change jobs? Get a raise? Have you made any big purchases? Bought or sold any stocks? Made a 1031 exchange on any real estate you own? Many of these substantial changes require notice to your spouse, so always let your attorney know when you are anticipating these things.

Likewise, your lawyer should ask for similar financial updates from your soon-to-be ex-spouse. Keeping current keeps both of you financially protected.

That's it for the art of "winning" in divorce. Now we are going to change gears slightly—though our focus will stay on strategy. In our next chapter we cover alternatives to a high-conflict divorce.

7

ALTERNATIVES TO A
HIGH-CONFLICT DIVORCE

Almost no one wants a divorce with drama. They're stressful, they're expensive, and they're toxic. The negativity they generate can linger for months, if not years, beyond the actual marital dissolution.

So, what makes a divorce high conflict?

Most high-conflict divorces end up in trial or get right up to the doorstep. Going to trial necessarily means you have exhausted all attempts at compromise and now require the state's power to resolve your personal issues. (At least some issues.) Many times, we can still settle most of these concerns.

However, there *are* times when some items just can't be agreed on. That's when going to trial comes into play. Note: While going to trial is always an option, there are risks involved. Going to trial necessarily means putting your fate—and perhaps your children's fate—in the hands of a judge who doesn't know you, doesn't really care about you, and will forget about you just as soon as their business with you is done.

If that sounds cold, that's because it is.

This is why I always consider trial to be a last resort. That said, *preparing* for trial is something I do with each and every client from the outset. (It's like having school fire drills. You practice and practice so that if and when a crisis comes, you are ready.) Basically, I want to be ready for all contingencies. Now, if you still think resolving your divorce in a trial is a good idea, here are specific disadvantages to consider:

- *It's inconvenient.* The court will determine the date and time you and your spouse are to appear, and you are obligated to comply. If this interferes with your business or a planned vacation, tough noogies. Want your day in court? This is it.

- *It can be intimidating or humiliating.* Court proceedings are a matter of public record. If you have any compunctions about airing your dirty linen in public, you're about to face your greatest fear. You probably won't get the level of attention of, say, a *Johnny Depp v. Amber Heard* (2022) or another salacious celebrity divorce proceeding, but if anyone wants to poke their nose into your private affairs, they'll be here for all the world to see. And you can't do a damned thing about it.

- *It's expensive.* When you go to court, attorneys' hours add up. Fast. Trials require your attorney, their associate(s), paralegal(s) and secretary(s) to spend substantial time preparing for the rules each judge sets out. Most judges are so specific about preparing and exhibiting evidence that it just takes a lot of time and effort and your money to get there.

- *It's contentious.* Trials are ripe for added conflict. It's baked into their DNA. If you have any notions about remaining friends with your ex, going to trial may dissuade you of those. One rarely emerges unscathed from such battles.

- *It's unpredictable.* When you negotiate a settlement, you retain some degree of control over how matters resolve, even if such resolutions are not wholly to your liking. This is not true in court. Here, the judge has total and final authority to impose whatever terms they see fit.

So, as I've been saying all along, you want to avoid trial—or at least a long, drawn-out trial—if at all possible. There are several ways you can do so. Let's focus on one now.

Mediated Settlement

We've discussed the benefits of prenups in previous chapters. I repeat this one for emphasis: With a thorough prenup, you can decide many terms of your divorce when you're calm, rational, and actually in love (one hopes). You can also eliminate the need to thrash things out when you are angry, upset, and out for blood.

However, if you don't have a prenup in place, a mediated settlement can be the next best thing. A mediated divorce is, as its name suggests, one in which a couple hires an impartial third party—the *mediator*—to help them work through their issues to arrive at a mutually agreeable settlement. Mediation can take three to four months or be as quick as the parties coming to an agreement.

Here are some specifics to consider. First, mediation privacy is the rule. This means neither of the parties can later call a mediator to testify in court. Why? The entire process is private and privileged. Even so, if you opt for mediation and it fails to resolve your conflict, you can still use information prepared in the process to continue litigation.

Personally, I am wary of turning to mediators. That's because just about anyone can hang out their shingle as a mediator with little formal training. If you are going the mediation route in your divorce, I highly recommend you also hire an advising attorney on an hourly retainer. (You should always consult a lawyer before signing *anything*, plus you can hire this person as your lawyer if the mediation goes south.)

The Private Judge Option

Beyond considering mediation, there are other options to high-stakes divorces. Utilizing a private judge is one. A private judge is someone you hire to perform the same role as a judge in family court, only it's done outside the public court system. This alternative is specifically permitted by the California State Constitution and the Code of Civil Procedure section 638(a), and while it can be used to adjudicate a wide range of civil cases, it is particularly popular in those involving divorce. In fact, about 25 percent of my clients choose to go this route.

Although private judges work outside the public court system, they are obliged to adhere to the same ethical standards as regular judges. Under Rule 1-710 of the California Rules of Professional Conduct, "a member who is serving as a temporary judge, referee, or court-appointed arbitrator, and is subject under the Code of Judicial Ethics to Canon 6D, shall comply with the terms of that canon." Failure to follow the code of ethics can result in any settlement you reach being challenged and ultimately overturned.

Note: private judges tend to be more expensive than mediators. (As of this writing, they tend to charge between $600 and $1,200 per hour compared to $250 to $500 for mediators.) This is because most private judges are, in fact, retired judges. They have actual law degrees, plus they bring decades of education, experience, and wisdom most mediators lack.

So why choose to have your divorce settled by a private judge rather than a mediator? There are benefits to opting for this smoother, simpler route to divorce resolution:

1. *As stated, most are retired judges.* They are *very* experienced in these matters, which means you're more likely to get a just and reasonable ruling.

2. *Their focus is greater.* They have specific experience with divorce law, whereas many mediators work in a broader area of civil litigation.

3. *Convenience.* Many private judges allow hearings to be held in a lawyer's office or even via video conferencing (e.g., Zoom).

4. *Privacy.* Like mediation, proceedings held with a private judge are, well, *private.* This can be a significant benefit to wealthy, high-profile individuals who would like to keep the display of their marital conflicts shielded from public eyes. (No Amber Heard insanity here!)

5. *Speed.* Divorces accomplished via a private judge tend to conclude much faster than going through the public court system and, as with mediation, a private judge's decision is legally binding. It's an actual ruling, not just a suggestion.

The Pros and Cons of Divorce Mediation

Let's spend some more time discussing mediation, which remains a popular way to settle a contested divorce. As with anything in life, mediation offers advantages and disadvantages over its alternatives. Here are the major pros and cons of this approach.

Pros

- *Cost.* Settlements accomplished via mediation tend to be less costly overall than those achieved in court.

- *Speed.* Mediation is usually a much faster process than going to trial. The average divorce takes fifteen months to two years to get through the public court system.

- *Amity.* The atmosphere during a mediation tends to be far less acrimonious than that in a civil trial. If you and your spouse wish to part amicably, mediation may offer the best chance for long-term success.

- *Convenience.* In most situations, you have more control over where and when you meet with your mediator—compared to scheduling time to appear in court.

- *Privacy.* Mediation is a private matter and, unlike a divorce trial, is never a matter of public record.

- *Satisfaction.* According to surveys, people who divorced through mediation report being more satisfied with the process than many who went to court.

Cons

- *Compromise.* Mediation is designed to arrive at a compromise. If your aim is to "win" and make your spouse "lose," a trial may be more to your liking.

- *Financial risk.* Unlike a trial, a mediator is not obligated to arrive at a final judgment. If the opposing parties refuse to cooperate, the entire mediation process can simply collapse, at which point the couple has no choice but to go to trial. In such a situation, you end up paying *twice*—first for the cost of the failed mediation and then for the cost of the trial itself. Trials, by contrast, are one-and-done. The judge *must* arrive at a final judgment.

- *Inexperience.* As I mentioned, some mediators do not have the requisite background/experience, which can lead to less-than-optimal outcomes. (I have had so many cases in which inexperienced mediators produced a poor agreement that led to more litigation and more pain for the parties involved.) Example: One couple spent $5,000 on a (faulty) mediator's agreement. The fiasco led both parties to each spend $500,000, plus appellate fees to resolve the matter.

CHOOSING A MEDIATOR

1. When choosing a mediator, make sure the person is also a licensed lawyer. A lawyer knows the ins and outs of family law and can explain the law to both parties.

2. Since a mediator's job is to gain agreement, I recommend getting an advising attorney as a sounding board. This latter individual will look after your rights and provide needed insights.

3. If needed, I may recommend retaining a forensic accountant to deal with more complex financial issues and some of the subtleties of Moore/Marsden (a calculation for dividing real property) and Van Camp or Pereira formulas.

The Mediation Experience Itself

Now let's drill down more on the mediation process. It's designed to allow two opposing spouses to reach an agreement over details of their divorce. This process is facilitated or mediated by an impartial third party with relevant training and experience in negotiating, diplomacy, and psychology.

Mediation usually takes place in an informal office setting but can, as is increasingly common, unfold online. The process occurs over multiple sessions. Note: You shouldn't go into your mediation blind. Before the formal mediation session ever begins, meet with your chosen mediator to review California divorce and child custody laws, learn your rights under California law, and review the likely timeline and cost of the mediation process.

Once all of this is understood and agreed to, you will meet with the mediator to review all your financial documents (tax returns, investment portfolio, property holdings, asset inventories, etc.) to determine all your joint and separate assets and liabilities. If everyone involved agrees to move ahead, the mediation itself can now begin.

This usually occurs in various phases:

1. *Initial meeting.* The objective here is to get everyone on the same page, or to at least get everyone to agree on what they disagree about. (This itself is a step in the right direction.) Once this foundation has been laid, the real negotiations can begin.

2. *Continued discussions.* You and your spouse will now meet with the mediator to gauge their feelings and ideas about the relative strengths and weaknesses of each side, as well as to establish a framework for what the final negotiated settlement *might* look like. In a series of follow-up discussions, you and the mediator

will work through each issue in contention until you come up with an offer you believe will be acceptable, if not attractive, to the other side. Depending on the mediator's strategy, this can be done on an issue-by-issue basis, or as a comprehensive package.

3. *Negotiations.* Once the mediator feels that an agreement is close, you and your spouse will be asked to again sit down together. (There's no reason to waste everyone's time if the sides are still far apart.) At this time, both parties can make their offers and counteroffers. Having come to know and understand each side's desires and rationales, the mediator will attempt to steer you and your spouse to a final settlement agreement.

4. *Settlement.* This is what everyone has been working toward. A final settlement will be drafted, reviewed by both sides, and made subject to legal review by each party's lawyer. If deemed acceptable, you and your spouse will sign the document and then submit it to the court, which will issue the final divorce judgment.

Understand that a settlement agreed to via mediation is a binding, legal contract. Once the settlement is signed, you can't have second thoughts, renege on a provision, or suddenly bring up additional issues for negotiation. You must get it right the first time. There's no divorce from your divorce. This is true for any stipulated judgment.

WHEN MEDIATION IS NOT APPROPRIATE

Mediation is not recommended for divorces involving charges of physical or emotional abuse. To be legitimate, a mediation must

continued

involve two parties who enter the proceeding on an equal footing and can make rational decisions on their own behalf. If one party feels threatened by the other or is uncomfortable in the other's presence, then these basic criteria are not met. In such a case, I believe going to court, with all the protections of the state in place, is the best, safest option.

Negotiating in Bad Faith: A Cautionary Tale

As with any negotiation, a successful mediation requires all parties operate in good faith. Going into a mediation thinking you can game the system or otherwise cheat your way to victory is likely to backfire.

Raymond and Eloise had agreed to settle their divorce through mediation. Going in, several issues were in dispute: what would happen to their four-bedroom house in Huntington Beach, ownership of a two-bedroom cabin in Big Bear, possession of a forty-two-foot cabin cruiser, and custody of their three school-aged children.

Early in the negotiations, the two agreed that Raymond would get the boat, which was worth close to $500,000. As it was community property, he would pay Eloise $250,000 to claim 100 percent ownership.

That out of the way, they started to talk about the house. While Raymond thought it would be best to sell it and split the proceeds, Eloise disagreed. "This is the only house the kids have ever known. They love it. They don't want to move."

Raymond demurred and said Eloise could keep the house, but she would have to pay him half of its $2 million value. Since he already owed her $250,000 for the boat, she could buy him out for just $750,000.

Eloise objected. She didn't want to pay Raymond *anything*.

"You keep the boat. I'll keep the house," she insisted.

Of course, this made no sense, as the home was worth four times the boat.

"Fine," Eloise finally relented. "I'll sell the house . . . if you sell the boat."

"But we already agreed on the boat."

Negotiations continued this way. The house. The boat. The vacation home. The kids. Every time they agreed to one point, she'd backtrack and change a condition for the next agreement. When the mediator realized what she was doing, she grew alarmed. Clearly, Eloise was screwing with Raymond for the sheer pleasure of it.

When called on it, she confessed without hesitation.

"I don't want him to get a damned thing," she said. "The guy's been a pain in my ass for fifteen years, and I want what's mine. I'm entitled to it."

"What you *feel* you deserve and what the State of California says you're entitled to are two different things," the mediator reminded her.

As one might have predicted, the mediation failed to produce a settlement and the case was forced to go to court. There, Eloise continued to play her head games. But the judge wasn't buying any of it, and she ended up getting far, far less than what she believed she was entitled to.

A Word about Mediators

"These aren't the droids you're looking for," wizened Obi-wan Kenobi calmly assures two suspicious Imperial Stormtroopers, his hand waving almost imperceptibly in the original 1977 *Star Wars*. Although the robots R2-D2 and C-3PO—for whom an all-points bulletin has been issued across the desert planet Tatooine—are clearly visible seated in the rear of young Luke Skywalker's battered landspeeder, the clueless Stormtroopers wave the party along.

This is a Jedi mind trick, now a staple of George Lucas's sprawling *Star Wars* universe. Through simple suggestion, Jedi Knights—wise in the ways of the Force—can subtly bend common folk to their will.

Mediators, although not carrying lightsabers or able to levitate rocks through sheer mental effort, often have a few mind tricks of their own. And divorcing couples entering mediation should be aware of them so as not to fall prey to such psychological manipulation.

These are the top five warning signs that you have a bad mediator:

1. Your mediator takes the other's side too much. (They should be straight down the middle.)

2. They cannot answer questions readily.

3. They come unprepared.

4. They are not a licensed lawyer.

5. They use psychological chicanery and emotional manipulation to affect the outcome.

Words and Phrases to Avoid in Court-Ordered Custody Mediation

If you are in court and have disputes over child custody, you are mandated to meet with a court mediator in family services prior to litigation. It's best to be prepared for this experience, especially the words you choose to speak.

There are many phrases and verbal tics that experienced divorce mediators and family law judges recognize as indicators of evasion, prevarication, or general irresponsibility. By knowing these in advance, you can avoid defaulting to them and thus maintain your credibility with the people who will determine the shape of your future existence.

The following are some of the most common no-no's you should avoid.

Saying "my kids." Using this singular possessive will force the ire of the judge, either overtly or subconsciously. In fact, I have, in court, heard judge after judge say, "So your husband/wife is nothing? You *share* these children." When referring to your offspring, always say "our kids" or "our children." Judges and mediators want to see that you recognize child-rearing as a *joint* effort.

Saying, "Custody should be fifty-fifty." When it comes to custody/visitation, you will be asked what you imagine the optimal schedule should be and why. Most parents, wanting to appear magnanimous, offer to split the difference by saying, "It should be fifty-fifty." But all this tells the mediator/judge is that you're looking at this like you would a business issue, calculating percentages. What you're *not* doing is thinking about the kids' interests. Instead of offering to split everything down the middle, you want to describe what the actual arrangement should look like: "I believe shared custody is ideal because they need both of us. We both have different talents and abilities we can use to help our children." This may trigger a follow-up question: "Describe what you mean by *shared custody*?" You could say, "One week with their mother and then one week with me, so we each have a chance to take them to schools, activities, and so on." Speaking this way demonstrates you recognize your spouse as a person and a vital part of your children's lives, not just as an interest that needs to be satisfied.

Speaking negatively about your spouse. Although divorces are, by nature, contentious, you never want to spend the custody hearing/ mediation bad-mouthing your spouse. In fact, you should prepare for such an appearance by coming up with between five and ten *good* things you can say about your soon-to-be-ex, especially related to child-rearing. (And, trust me, you *will* be asked to do so.) There is one exception to this rule, and that is if you believe your spouse is abusive or otherwise represents a *physical* threat to your children's safety. In such a case, be prepared to support your claims with evidence, such as police reports, doctor's notes, reports from Child Protective Services, or similar documentation. Your word alone is not likely to be sufficient to sway a judge and may, in fact, backfire.

Dress for Success in Mediation and in Court

The following can apply to either the mediation setting or the trial itself. It's been almost fifty years since John T. Malloy's book *Dress for Success* published. In the half century since, work fashion has changed significantly. (Especially for post-COVID remote workers!) But the idea that you'll be judged—sometimes harshly—based on your wardrobe remains as valid today as it was during the Gerald Ford Administration. In fact, if the adage "the clothes make the man (or woman)" is any indication, the sentiment probably goes as far back as humanity itself.

It's certainly true in the world of *juris prudence*. When arguing before a judge, an attorney is expected to wear a nice suit, have polished shoes, and be impeccably groomed. To show up in court wearing jeans, sneakers, and an open-collared shirt is tantamount to legal malpractice. Likewise, plaintiffs and defendants must clean up as well before an appearance. How you *look* will make an impression and bias your mediator/judge for or against you long before you or your attorney ever utter your first word.

For court appearances, mediations, and depositions, both women and men should dress as if they are going to their most important job interview. Women should dress conservatively. No miniskirts, no low-cut stuff. Don't think you will impress the judge by dressing provocatively. You want the air of legitimacy and to be taken seriously. Women should wear an outer layer like a jacket or blazer. I recommend red (it shows strength and confidence). You can't go wrong with dressing up. But there are times when I recommend not dressing up super fancy—like don't wear a $25,000 watch when we are discussing money. Men will never go wrong with a suit and tie. Initial impressions are usually quick and subconscious. I suggest wearing a navy suit (sincere blue), white shirt, and conservative tie. Shined shoes.

Now that we know alternatives for high-conflict divorce, in the next chapter, we explore court-ordered mediation as well as other issues surrounding divorces involving minor children.

8

CHILDREN AND DIVORCE

A divorce is *always* traumatic. Mental health experts will tell you that a divorce is as psychologically damaging as a death in the family.[1] This is not surprising, as divorce *is* a form of death. It's the death *of* a family. It's the death of what was intended to be a permanent relationship. It's the death of a future that will never be.

But as painful as a divorce is to the parting spouses, it's even more so when children are involved. (This is true regardless of a child's age.) Divorce has an impact on infants. It has an impact on teenagers. It even has an impact on grown adults!

The sections that follow summarize how mental experts describe the impact of divorce on minor children by age group.[2]

Infants (birth to eighteen months). Newborns obviously have no concept of marriage and divorce; nor can they discuss any emotional turmoil they may be experiencing. However, babies can sense tension, anxiety, and anger in their parents, react with fear to the sound of fighting, and know when daily routines are being upset. They may react to this negativity by being chronically cranky, having erratic sleep patterns, being unusually clingy when around new people, and being prone to fits of anger and crying. Many infants caught up in the maelstrom of divorce suffer from delayed physical, mental, and emotional development—delays that can linger for years.

Toddlers (eighteen months to three years). Children at this stage are beginning to acquire self-awareness, understand they are separate from their parents, and usually see themselves as the center of the universe (and therefore responsible for everything that happens around them). When toddlers view their parents breaking apart, they may conclude they are the cause and experience the guilt that goes with such culpability. They may cry frequently and demand constant attention and affirmation. They may also resist such developmental milestones as toilet training and sleeping alone at night. They may also demand to stay in their infant cribs rather than graduating to a traditional bed.

Preschoolers (three to six years). These children have acquired a functional vocabulary but still have difficulty processing and expressing their emotions. They may understand the concept of divorce in the most abstract sense but, not having any practical experience with permanent separation from a loved one, cannot imagine what that actually entails for *them*. Like their younger counterparts, they are likely to see themselves as the cause of their parents' problems and view themselves negatively as a result. Preschoolers whose parents are in the midst of a divorce may be prone to rebellious misbehavior, may resist discipline, and may even become physically violent.

Grammar-school-age children (six to eleven years). At this age, most children are binary thinkers. This means they see the world in terms of black and white, light and dark, good guys and bad guys. If, after years of living in a stable home, their parents divorce, grammar-school-age children are apt to align themselves with one parent or the other, designate one as "good" and the other as "bad." Or they might fantasize about "rescuing" their parents' failed marriage *Parent Trap*–style. Unable to deal with their boiling emotions and insecurities, boys may lash out physically, get into fights with schoolmates, and damage property. Girls, on the other hand, may withdraw from school and friendships, fall into deep depressions, and may even begin to practice self-harm (e.g., cutting). With both boys and girls, it's not unusual for their schoolwork to suffer.

Teenagers (eleven to eighteen years). As bad as the impact of divorce can be on grammar-school-age children, the effects on teenagers are even stronger. Adolescence alone is a difficult time for most people, but compound the effects of hormone overload and extreme social pressures with the stresses of marital dissolution and the crumbling of household security, and you have a recipe for disaster. Although most teens have the intellectual capacity to understand and perhaps even accept the idea of their parents breaking up, it's not at all unusual for them to deal with the emotional discomfort via drugs, sexual adventurism, extreme risk-taking, violence, and self-harm. Their academic performance is bound to slide, as is their emotional and social development. Parents going through a divorce need to look for signs of depression in their teen children and take immediate action if their kids discuss thoughts of suicide.

So how do you handle children while you are going through a divorce? How do you keep your divorce from becoming *their* divorce? And how is your approach to your children likely to affect custody and visitation rights when your divorce is final?

Regardless of your children's ages, you must work to keep your personal differences as far from them as possible. Do *not* fight in front of them. Do not even let them *hear* you fight when they're in another room. Establish and maintain a daily schedule regarding waking, mealtimes, play times, school, homework, baths, book reading, and bedtimes to give them a sense of security and predictability. Also give them plenty of hugs and personal time. If they are old enough to understand, explain in simple terms why you and your spouse have decided to live apart, and emphasize that they remain loved and that the divorce is in no way their fault. Paint them a mental picture of what their future life is likely to look like in positive terms. Throughout this long and difficult process, make your kids, not your divorce, the center of your life.

When considering divorce, both parents should meet with a well-qualified child psychologist and discuss the way to communicate with their kids. I recommend *Helping Your Kids Cope with Divorce the Sandcastles Way: Based on the Program Mandated in Family Courts Nationwide*, by M. Gary Neuman and Patricia Romanowski.

TALKING TO YOUR KIDS ABOUT AN IMPENDING DIVORCE

Do:

- Be honest when answering questions.

- Give age-appropriate answers.

- Let your children know what life will be like after the divorce.

- Emphasize that the divorce is final.

- Reassure your kids.

- Talk well about the other parent.

- Be available.

- Communicate stability, but don't be afraid to show emotion.

Definitely do *not*:

- Speak poorly about the other parent.

- Blame your kids or your spouse.

- Make your kids choose between parents.

- Use your children as pawns.

- Limit access to your kids for ridiculous reasons.

- Bad-mouth the other parent via text or email.

- Use your children as the conduit for adult communications.

The Case of the Manipulative Mother

Tom and Susan were in their late forties when they decided to divorce. They had two children: a boy, age fourteen, and a girl, age ten.

Susan was notorious for trying to play the kids off against their dad. She would schedule his visitations during times when Tom had important out-of-town business trips so, when he couldn't show up, she could tell the kids they were not his priority. When their son asked for a new snowboard, she told him she couldn't afford one because, although their dad was "rich," he was too cheap to pay them sufficient child support. She frequently indulged the kids in ways she knew Tom would object to just to paint him as the bad guy.

Because Tom had started dating again (as had she), she would press the kids for information about their dad's sex life—especially wildly inappropriate info—asking for details no mom should ever ask their kids.

She also sent Tom long, profanity-laced emails in which she bad-mouthed his entire family. She threatened to tell his business partner every terrible thing he ever told her privately.

When the judge overseeing the couple's divorce learned about Susan's manipulations, he granted primary custody to Tom, citing Susan's bad behavior and hostility, which he deemed detrimental to the children. He said it would not be in the children's best interest to be raised in such an emotionally toxic environment.

The strategy Susan had devised to alienate her kids from their dad had, in fact, just the *opposite* effect. Had she not been so manipulative, she may have had a better chance of getting the outcome she so desired.

Yes, Divorce Affects Grown Children, Too

So far, we have only discussed issues regarding how divorce affects minor children. This is because, legally, children eighteen years old and up don't figure into the equation. Once children turn eighteen and have graduated high school, the law considers them grown adults responsible for their own well-being.

There is no such thing as a child custody arrangement for a twenty-year-old.

But don't let legalities fool you. Grown children *are* affected by divorce, regardless of their age. And more and more of them are having to learn to cope with this painful experience. In the twenty-five years between 1990 and 2015, the divorce rate for people fifty and over *doubled*, forcing an unprecedented number of grown children to deal with the idea of coming from a broken family. The reasons for this sharp increase in so-called gray divorce remain a matter of debate, but we can assume that women's growing economic self-sufficiency had much to do with it. (As noted, most divorces are instigated by women.)

There are many ways adults are affected by their parents' divorce, including:

- *Economic anxiety.* Although they may be legal adults, people ages nineteen to twenty-five are often still heavily dependent financially on their parents, especially if they're in college or graduate school. A young man or woman whose parents suddenly split may fear the support they've so far taken for granted may now be jeopardized.

- *Family politics.* Family occasions like birthdays, anniversaries, and holiday get-togethers can become logistical nightmares if parents not only live separately but remain hostile toward each other postdivorce. Things become even more complicated if the divorced parents remarry—which is often the case—and suddenly the grown kids have a whole new set of extended families to which they must adjust.

- *Self-doubt.* When a divorce occurs between parents of children who are now old enough to seriously contemplate marriage, or may even be married themselves, it can trigger lingering doubt about the validity of the entire institution. The kids may look at their parents—whom they have likely idealized their entire lives—and figure, "If they couldn't make it work, how can I?" Modeling isn't something parents do just for young kids. How parents behave, even in late adulthood, becomes a psychological template their children may feel compelled to imitate, even if only subconsciously.

Child Custody Court-Ordered Mediation

In the previous chapter, we talk about private mediation as an alternative to a public trial. This was *voluntary* mediation. You enter such mediation *by choice* and have the option of terminating it if you and your spouse fail to come to terms. No one forces you into this kind of mediation. It's an alternative that if not wholly preferable, is certainly the least objectionable.

But there is another kind of mediation: court-ordered mediation. This occurs when minor children are involved, you and your spouse cannot agree on a custody/visitation plan, and you have decided to go to trial. In this case, before you go before a judge, you *must* enter this type of mediation. It's the law (at least in California).

In court-ordered mediation, the parties sit down with a mental health professional who helps them talk through their disagreements with the aim of developing a parenting plan both can agree on. These meetings take place at the family court and are restricted to child custody and visitation issues *only*. Other matters, such as spousal support and property division, are not on the table. Some counties require parents to complete an orientation before mediation; check with your attorney or superior court to find out the rules in your area.

Recommending versus Non-recommending

In some California counties, the mediator in a child-custody dispute will make a formal recommendation to the judge on how any custody/visitation dispute should be resolved. Such counties are called *recommending counties*. In Southern California, San Diego County is a recommending county.

In other counties, the mediator will attempt to bring the parents to an agreement but, if an agreement is not reached, will go no further. No recommendation is made to the court. Such counties are called *non-recommending counties*. In Southern California, both Los Angeles and Orange counties are non-recommending counties.

If you live in San Diego or another recommending county, you want to be professional and show your parenting capabilities to your mediator as much as possible. Be polite, respectful, accommodating, and even deferential. Always talk about how much you love your kids and how involved you are in their lives. Behaving in this way improves your chances of getting a recommendation that leans in your favor.

On the other hand, if you live in Los Angeles County or Orange County, such interfacing offers no payoff. Even if the mediator thinks you're the greatest parent since Ward and June Cleaver, it'll make no difference. Your judge will make all child custody and visitation decisions without the mediator's input unless you come to an agreement. I tell clients to show up and be polite. I have had a couple of occasions where the mediator thought the toxicity between the parents rose to such a noxious level that they actually reported this to the court.

QUICK TIPS FOR PARENTS GOING INTO COURT-ORDERED MEDIATION

- Learn if mediators in your county make recommendations to the court; if so, be careful to not say or do anything in mediation that could hurt your request for custody.

- Meet with an attorney beforehand. If not possible, prepare thoroughly on your own so you come knowing where you're willing to compromise.

continued

- Be responsible and respectful. Arrive punctually, dress neatly, and don't interrupt.

- Remember your time is limited. Make points succinctly and focus on crucial topics.

- Keep your kids' interests and needs at the forefront of the discussion rather than your own.

- Don't raise your voice or get angry.

- Try not to speak negatively about the other parent.

- Keep an open mind.

- Be honest. But honestly, don't speak bad about your ex.

- Take notes so you can remember what was said.

- Don't feel pressured into agreeing to anything you will regret.

- Be forthcoming with any questions you have.

How to Psychologically Prepare for Court-Ordered Mediation

Having a successful court-ordered child custody and visitation mediation often requires one to undergo what was once popularly called a major attitude adjustment. Any long-held sentiments, opinions, and expectations you may have held to this point must be recalibrated to reflect the new reality you are about to enter.

Up until now, your divorce has likely focused on the *differences* you have with your spouse. You've been thinking about how to take your marriage apart. Now not only is it time to be thinking about accommodation, but you must put someone else's interests ahead of your own—namely, your children's.

Before going into court-ordered mediation, here are some ways to prepare yourself psychologically for the challenge ahead:

- *Become a Zen master.* In American popular culture, a Zen master is in total control of their emotions, a person who can stay calm and serene even amid chaos. Drawn from actual practitioners of Buddhist meditative traditions, the Zen master inspired such fictional characters as *Star Trek's* Mr. Spock and *The Karate Kid's* Mr. Miyagi. When preparing for court-ordered mediation or a court appearance, it helps to keep the Zen master character in mind. Despite how you might *actually* feel, you want to appear tranquil, relaxed, and quietly confident. The *last* thing you want to do is come off as loud, combative, angry, or even whiney. If things get tense, just shut your eyes, breathe deeply, and never let 'em see you sweat.

- *Don't involve the kids.* Only do this if you do it together with a spouse who also thinks of the children first. Obviously, you're not going to defer to the wishes of a five-year-old, but listening to your children and acknowledging their fears and desires can not only help steer subsequent discussions in a positive direction but also help alleviate some of the young ones' anxieties.

- *Think "teamwork or co-parenting."* This is important from the court's perspective. When you initially got married, you became part of a unit. You and your spouse were a couple. Your interests were aligned. Now that you're getting divorced, the temptation is to think of yourself as single again. But if children are involved, you must reject that mindset. You may no longer live with your spouse, but you continue to share joint responsibilities for your children's upbringings. When it comes to your kids, you and your spouse are still a team, and you should approach mediation from this perspective.

- *Be nice to your ex-spouse.* This is probably the toughest part of mediation preparation. Until now, your attitude toward this person has likely been highly negative. You've only been able to think about what's *wrong* with the individual you're preparing to divorce. Now you must turn that around. You have to start thinking about what's *good* about your former significant other—particularly when it comes to co-parenting. Not only will this put you in a better, less combative mood when you enter mediation, but chances are your mediator will specifically ask you to discuss your spouse's positive aspects. By thinking about these in advance, you'll be prepared to respond without hesitation. (And the mediator will like that.)

If the court is in a reporting county, the mediator will make a child custody and a visitation recommendation to a judge who many times will simply rubber stamp that recommendation. As we know from our discussions throughout this book concerning strategy, in court-ordered mediation, as in so many other aspects of life, preparation is everything. This is why before I send any of my clients to meet with a mediator, especially in a reporting county, I stage at least one mock mediation. Here I play the part of the mediator and run the client through a series of likely questions and challenges. (This is very much the way political candidates prepare for debates, by rehearsing their responses to likely questions until they become rote.)

Such rehearsals put the client at ease when the real mediation begins. After all, nothing is as frightening as fear of the unknown. Rehearsal also helps me spot and correct poor or inconsistent responses.

Mediators, like judges, have been down this path innumerable times, and they tend to be pretty good at spotting lies and insincerity. (At least they *think* they are.)

As your lawyer, it's my job to look for *tells* signaling to a judge or mediator that you are being less than truthful and then help you devise the most positive, constructive response to a question while remaining honest.

Your Kids Are Your Job

Raising children is a full-time pursuit. This is true even if you're a working parent who already *has* a full-time job. To score points in a custody dispute, you must show your dedication to your children and their well-being is absolute.

If your kids are of school age, this means:

- Knowing the names of all your kids' teachers

- Knowing your kids' school schedules, grades, and homework content

- Knowing the names and personalities of their friends

- Knowing your kids' likes, dislikes, and outside interests

What are your kids' favorite toys? Books? Movies? TV shows? Foods? Knowing these details shows you are an attentive parent. Make sure you have spent plenty of time with your kids on evenings and weekends. You should be able to describe, *in detail*, the places you've gone together and the activities you've shared.

You can't plan on getting primary custody or a co-parenting relationship just out of ego or to score points against your ex. As I've said before, your children are not pawns to be advanced or sacrificed to help you score a win. If you don't want to be a full-time parent when called on to be so, then speak up. I suspect the court will be happy to accommodate you.

Why Bad-Mouthing Your Spouse Is a Bad Idea

I have already mentioned that parents going through a divorce should not criticize, demean, blame, undercut, denigrate, malign, vilify, disparage, belittle, or otherwise bad-mouth each other in front of their children. There are several specific reasons to suppress this temptation—both for your children's sakes and for your own.

Talking down one's spouse can have profound psychological effects on children. First, since kids recognize that they represent an amalgam of *both* parents, they will figure that, if there is something fundamentally wrong with Mom or Dad, then there is probably something equally deficient in *them*.

Next, having a parent portrayed as deeply flawed makes kids feel insecure about *themselves*. Such condemnation necessarily undermines the other spouse's moral authority, and thus their ability to discipline or otherwise control the kids when in their custody.

If Mom or Dad is a selfish, erratic, narcissistic jerk, why should the kids do what they say? Finally, it forces kids to take sides, to choose one parent over another, something no child should ever have to do. No doubt your kids love you and your spouse equally—they're *supposed* to and they *want* to—and they are going to feel horrible about doing so if you tell them Mom/Dad is an irredeemable jerk. Don't put them in that position.

As bad as talking down one's spouse is for kids, it's just as bad for you. Kids behave the way they're treated. If you come off as angry, negative, and spiteful, you're going to have kids who are angry, negative, and spiteful. (Good luck corralling *those* wild mustangs.)

Spend your time grousing about how bad Mom/Dad is, and the kids are going to start thinking there is something wrong with *you*. Which further undermines *your* authority. And when word gets to the court that you've been denigrating your spouse in this manner—and believe me, it will—all your vitriol is going to backfire.

After all, courts want children raised in positive, safe, and stable homes. They will remove children from those they consider toxic. So, if you think bad-mouthing your spouse will help you win primary custody, this is not a good plan. Just the opposite will happen.

Want to be seen as a model parent? Play nice. If you have nothing nice to say, say it anyway. In the end, you'll be glad you did.

The Case of the Detailed Dad

Although Jim and Meg managed to stay married for ten years, they had very different lifestyles. Jim was an entrepreneur who worked from home. Much of his success could be traced to his personal discipline and devotion to detail.

He awoke every day at precisely 5:30 a.m., weekends included. He went to bed at exactly 10:10 every night. And no matter how busy he was, he always quit work at exactly 5:00 p.m., after which he would play with their three young children, make them dinner, bathe them, and put them to bed.

His wife, Meg, was Jim's mirror opposite. She had little interest in the children. Not working, she spent most days out of the house shopping with friends or hanging out at the local country club. When she *was* home, she spent a *lot* of time on the phone while Jim attended to the young ones.

Shortly after their ten-year anniversary, Jim and Meg decided to divorce.

Jim became my client. For reasons Jim couldn't explain, Meg asked for primary custody. In the temporary child custody hearing—a hearing before a judge that occurs when a divorce process commences—Meg's attorney argued that Jim spent many weeks out of town on business, which was true, and so it was in the kids' best interest to be assigned to their mother.

The judge appeared to be swayed by this information. But then it was time for my cross-examination.

I had earlier advised Jim to keep a log documenting the hours he spent with his kids. And Jim being Jim, he did so with the specificity of Charles Darwin detailing the mating habits of the Galapagos tortoise. I presented this log, which covered the previous nine months, to the judge. Meg's lawyer had not advised her to document anything, and so she had no competing narrative to offer.

Based on Jim's demonstrable commitment to spending time with his kids, the court granted him primary custody. Such an arrangement was, the court believed, in the children's best interest.

This was not a ruling I was going to argue.

Can You Move Away?

Many clients ask me: If I get shared or even primary custody of my kids, does this mean I'm trapped? Can I move to a different town or even a different state without violating the terms of my custody agreement?

Obviously, a key factor in this question is how *far* you intend to move and how such a move is likely to affect your spouse's ability to share in child-rearing responsibilities. If you're planning to move across town, that probably won't be an issue. Moving from, say, Orange County to Los Angeles County becomes more problematic. Moving from California to New York—or the UK? Now that's definitely a matter for the courts.

In determining whether to allow a divorced parent with primary custody rights to move out of its jurisdiction, the court will apply what are called LaMusga factors (pronounced La Mushe), which arose from the 2014 case *Marriage of LaMusga*, in which a divorced mother asked for a change in custody orders so she could move from California to Ohio to pursue a career opportunity.

When considering modifying a custody order, the court will look at the following factors:

- The reason for the proposed move. (Is it legitimate or just a ploy to frustrate your ex-spouse?)

- The distance of your proposed move.

- Your children's age(s).

- How the move will affect your children's need for stability and consistency.

- Your children's current relationship with both parents.

- How well the parents have been able to cooperate in the raising of your children.

- Your children's wishes. (If they are mature enough to understand and evaluate the impact of the proposed move.)

Bottom line: if the person proposing the move can satisfy the court that (1) the move is legitimate and (2) the move is in the children's best interests, the court is likely to approve such a change in the original custody agreement.

The Case of the Furious Father

When Albert discovered his wife, Nicole, had been cheating on him, he was furious and demanded a divorce. He was even more enraged when Nicole announced she was moving from Southern California to suburban Atlanta to marry her lover—and intended to take their two daughters with her.

In court, Albert was unable to hide his bitterness and enmity from the judge who, not surprisingly, became concerned with the man's emotional stability. Albert's frequent outbursts and use of demeaning invectives against his ex-wife convinced the court that, while separating children from their father is never easy or desirable, it was still in their best interest to move cross-country with their mom.

Had Albert been able to control his temper and present himself as a strong, stable, and necessary partner in his children's upbringing, the result might have been different. This is why, in a custody dispute, it is always critical to comport yourself as your ex's partner with the children, rather than his or her adversary.

The Wonderful World of RFOs

Everyone knows what a trial is. You go to the courthouse. You watch as lawyers argue your case before a judge. The judge then renders a verdict.

RFOs are different. RFO stands for Request for Orders, and they are motions—requests—for a specific decision regarding a specific issue, usually something timely and urgent. For example, temporary child custody questions need to be resolved immediately upon separation. An RFO can resolve this while the parties wait for the actual trial to begin. The same goes for other timely matters, such as who gets to occupy the house, who pays whose temporary spousal support, and so on. It's like taking the entire divorce and slicing it into tiny pieces. Another way to describe it is "death by a thousand cuts."

In family law, RFOs are 90 percent of what we do. We take them *very* seriously. Why? Because they set a precedent for the final divorce decree. Courts are reluctant to relitigate issues on which they have already ruled. Judges look at whatever constitutes the status quo and figure, "If it ain't broke, don't fix it." As a result, if an RFO gives you primary custody of the kids, chances are you'll keep it in the final decree. So, long before we go to trial, we want to get as many questions as possible resolved through RFOs. (The more victories we notch through the RFO process, the bigger our win is likely to be in the final decree.)

The Case of the Magnanimous Mom

Now let's see an RFO in action. Kim and Larry had three kids ten and under. Although she had a CPA license, Kim hadn't worked full time since her children were born. Larry, an attorney, was the household's primary breadwinner.

When the two decided to divorce, I filed an RFO on Kim's behalf to resolve a variety of urgent issues ranging from temporary custody/ visitation, child and spousal support, control of certain assets, and attorney's fees. Kim, who was now working part-time from home, asked for a seventy-thirty custody split. She believed she had the time and bandwidth to give her kids the attention they needed. Her husband, Larry, wanted to make the arrangement fifty-fifty, even though his work as a lawyer kept him away from home many evenings and weekends. Although I advised Kim to stand her ground, she didn't want to make waves and, believing that any temporary arrangement was, indeed, *temporary*, acquiesced to Larry's request.

A year and a half later, when their case finally went to trial, Kim again asked for a seventy-thirty custody arrangement. But the judge looked at the fifty-fifty plan from the temporary orders that the RFO had established and asked, "How is this arrangement working? Any problems?" Since we couldn't argue that the fifty-fifty plan had failed— because it hadn't—the judge decided to maintain the status quo and granted them joint custody. *Permanently.*

Should You Wait until the Kids Are Grown to Divorce?

"You should stay together for the sake of the kids."

This is advice people often give parents who are contemplating divorce. Yes, divorce can be hard on children. But are dysfunctional families better for kids just because they stay intact?

Experts disagree on this question. Some say a stable home with both parents present is always a better environment for children, regardless of whether their parents actually get along.[3] Others contend that a home in which the parents are either fighting constantly or are coldly hostile to one another can be worse in the long term than a divorce. Children, they insist, need to see that their parents love and are devoted to each other to feel loved themselves.

Speaking from experience, I can only tell you that, among my clients, most of those who waited until their children were grown and out of the house to divorce regretted their decision. Waiting years—or even decades—to make a life change for which they've been desperate made them feel like they wasted a large and important part of their lives. They don't believe their children benefitted from having miserable parents. I see this same shampoo, rinse, and repeat scenario often play out with their own kids who often look back at their unhappy childhoods as a factor for their marital strife.

Should Your Child Have an Attorney?

Most divorces involve only two lawyers, one for each spouse. However, in high-conflict cases when neither side can be fully trusted to advocate for the children's best interests, the court may appoint its own counsel to represent the kids. This individual is known as the minor's counsel.

Under California law, a minor's counsel is considered appropriate if:

- There is high conflict or extended legal history between the parents.
- The dispute is causing the child stress.
- There is information available about the child's best interests that is not likely to be presented by either parent.
- There are claims of child abuse or neglect.
- Either or both parents may be incapable of providing a stable, safe, and secure environment for the child.

- There are special issues that a minor's counsel can provide insight into for the court.

- The court believes independent representation is best.

The minor's counsel can speak to the kids privately, without either parent present, plus will have access to normally confidential information such as medical records and school records, as well as court-sanctioned access to teachers, doctors, therapists, friends, and other people in the children's lives. The idea is to present the court with a full picture of the children's circumstances independent of what the parents might say.

Personally, I am skeptical of minor's counsels. They tend to be trained in the law but know little about actual child psychology. They don't know when kids are lying to them or exaggerating a situation (this happens a *lot*) and are easily manipulated by clever children.

As an alternative to a minor's counsel, I usually advocate for the appointment of a child psychologist. A trained, experienced child psychologist is better equipped to determine when children are telling the truth. They are also better at evaluating the quality of individual parent-child relationships than a minor's counsel and can make more qualified custody recommendations to the court.

There are two primary situations when the appointment of a child psychologist is appropriate: standard custody evaluations and therapy.

Standard custody evaluations. The court appoints an expert to evaluate the children, the home environment, and parents to give a court a professional recommendation as to the appropriate custody arrangement. (This is called an Evidence Code, Section 730 Custody Evaluation.) The cost of such an evaluation can vary from $7,500 up to $50,000 and be apportioned in any manner based on the parties' financial situations.

Therapy. Sometimes courts will order children to undergo therapy by a child psychologist to deal with the emotional difficulties resulting from contentious parents, emotional or physical abuse, trauma, and so on. Again, the costs of this can be apportioned in any manner based on the parties' financial situations.

At this point in your divorce, either you and your spouse have come to an agreement on property division and child custody—or you haven't. If any issues remain unresolved, you have no choice but to go to court. If you think things have been difficult up to this point, hang on. You ain't seen nothin' yet.

9

TRIAL

The big-picture idea of this chapter is this: everything you say or do in court is either building or eroding trust.

If your attempts at a negotiated divorce settlement fail, you will take your case to court. Here, amid the hallowed halls of our nation's justice system, you will try your case before a judge. Their ruling will have the force of law. Although divorce trials are common tropes in popular entertainment, they are, statistically speaking, quite rare. Only about a small percentage of all divorces ever end up in trial. To go to trial means a couple's conflicts are so extreme and intractable there is simply no other way to resolve them but through the force of the state.

If that sounds serious—it is.

There are good reasons why most people prefer to settle divorces via negotiation or mediation rather than go to court. Trials are expensive. Their outcomes are unpredictable. But perhaps most unnerving of all, when you go to court, you, as a litigant, lose all control over the process. Once a trial starts, all you can do is sit and stew while the lawyers battle like jousting knights of old. Yes, you will have a chance to testify on your own behalf, but any pleasure you may take in having your day in court may be dashed once you've been subjected to withering cross-examination by opposing counsel.

Trials are no fun—for you. I am at home in the courtroom. If you want someone to fight your battle, I will be that guy. All I ask is that you listen to my recommendations and settle what we can prior to trial. So let's take a look at what you—or, rather, your attorney—can do to increase your chances for a positive outcome.

Deposition Do's and Don'ts

Before trial, the attorneys for both parties will generally hold depositions. A deposition resembles witness testimony in a trial. The deponent—the person being deposed—swears an oath to tell the truth, the whole truth, and nothing but the truth under penalty of perjury.

A deposition is a question-and-answer session handled outside the courtroom, typically at your attorney's office. Every word is taken down by a court reporter and transcribed for potential future use in court. Importantly, all the responses are under oath, meaning a deponent must respond under penalty of perjury—just like court. (As divorce is a civil matter.)

Technically part of a case's discovery process, a deposition is designed to perform two functions:

1. Establish the facts of the case

2. Determine if the deponent will make a good or bad witness

In a divorce, three types of witnesses are generally deposed:

1. *The interested parties.* This means you, your spouse, and if you
    have any, your kids.

2. *Outside experts.* These can include accountants, psychologists,
    vocational evaluators, law enforcement officers, and so on.

3. *Third-party witnesses.* Think: friends, relatives, professional
    associates, domestic help, or anyone else who can provide rel-
    evant information about you or your spouse regarding how
    you treat your children, substance abuse, domestic violence,
    and so on. (Someone who speaks positively toward you is
    considered a "friendly" witness. One who speaks against you
    is considered a "hostile" witness.)

As for your own testimony, remember the maxim that everything
you say or do in this deposition is to build trust, not destroy it. You
want to be very intentional about how you present yourself.

What follows are some simple rules for surviving depositions.

Don't Be So Helpful

It's not your job to explain yourself. When you do so, you help the
other side. Saying more allows them to use the info against you. Take
this exchange, for example:

Question: Do you have bank accounts at Bank of America?

Answer: Checking accounts?

This person emphasized the word "checking" in such a way that it begs
the follow-up question, "What kinds of accounts do you have?" To

which the party might admit they have a brokerage account—which may not help their case.

Listen to the *Exact* Question

It's okay to ask for a repeat. It's fine to say, "I don't understand the question." If you do answer it—it will be *presumed* you understood it, so be sure that when you answer, you know exactly what they are asking.

Know That There Are Different Types of Answers

Types of answers include the following.

Unqualified. Yes or no questions. Example: "Do you have an account at Bank of America?" The answer is either yes or no.

Qualified. Could be a best estimate. Example: "When did you start your business?" There could be an exact answer, but you may not know it for sure. A good way to answer this would be, "To the best of my knowledge, it was approximately November 15." You are giving two qualifying responses. By doing this, you can still be wrong by a reasonable percentage, but you acknowledge your own fallibility. This helps with your perception in court.

Speculative. This is just guessing. I never want my client to guess because it could be used against you. For example, say a client took $100,000 out of an IRA last January. Here's the correct way to deal with this:

Question: Did you withdraw $100,000 from your retirement account?

Answer: Yes.

Question: When did you do this?

Answer: I'm not sure.

Question: Give me your best estimate.

Answer: My best estimate would be last spring, but I can't be sure without seeing statements. I simply don't recall.

Now, here's the incorrect way to deal with this:

Question: Did you withdraw $100,000 out of your retirement account?

Answer: Yes.

Question: When did you do this?

Answer: March 1.

Question: Okay, but it says here that you actually withdrew the monies in January of that year. Do you want to restate your answer?

Answer: Oh, yes. You must be right. I guess I got the dates wrong.

Note: both parties responded, but the latter could hurt their case. How? Client B speculated the answer that ended up being wrong, potentially harming credibility. (Remember the axiom at the start of this chapter!) Without a qualifier and instead asserting a "fact" that wasn't true, this could harm their standing before the court.

Don't Try to Anticipate Questions

People often try to adjust their answers based on where they *think* the other side is going. This is a mistake. Don't get ahead of the questions. By doing so, all you're doing is giving ammunition to the other side. Let's say a client has done something they should not have done, like taking $100,000 out of retirement without telling the other side.

> **Question:** Were you in San Francisco of March last year?

> **Bad answer:** I know where you're going with this. You think I stayed at the Ritz with my girlfriend, but I was there for business.

You are being asked about something that could be banal, but by trying to anticipate the question, you have now opened yourself up to a whole new line of questioning.

Remember That the Truth Is Always the Best Answer

When the court finds that you have not been fully honest, even about a seemingly small, trivial matter, they may never believe you again. It's better to fully expose yourself, warts and all, than be considered a liar.

Depositions versus Trials

As noted previously, depositions are primarily information-gathering exercises. They help attorneys determine what evidence they will eventually use at trial. They also enable each side to formulate a plan of attack against the other. Trials, on the other hand, are platforms in which pieces of evidence are weighed against each other to ultimately establish a final narrative/verdict. In the depositions, we get to hear each side's story. In the trial, a judge must decide which story carries more weight.

Presentation, while vital in a courtroom setting, is far less so in a deposition. Witnesses can dress casually in a deposition but must look their best in a courtroom. In a trial, a witness who speaks hesitantly, stumbles over words, sighs a lot, or rolls their eyes at questions can kill a case. Such failings are far less damaging in a deposition where the resulting written transcript is unlikely to reflect these issues. Unless taken by video.

Finally, the breadth of information covered in depositions tends to be broad. Personally, I object far less often in depositions than I do in court. During a trial, I try to keep the opposition's evidence to a minimum. In a deposition, it's just the opposite, as at this early stage I'm eager to see all the ammunition the enemy might use against me.

During your deposition, both your attorney and opposing counsel will be studying you closely to determine how credible you are likely to be in court. As you speak, they will judge your performance against the following scorecard:

1. Do you talk too much? (1 point for yes)

2. Do you have a need to explain yourself? (1 point for yes)

3. Do you roll your eyes? (1 point for yes)

4. Do you laugh inappropriately? (1 point for yes)

5. Do you shake your head when you hear a lie? (1 point for yes)

Score Analysis

Score of 1 = Not good but you can fix this.

Score of 2 = You need practice.

Score of 3 = Professional witness coach required.

Score of 4–5 = Intervention needed. Danger zone ahead.

So now that the depositions are over, it's time to prepare for court. Buckle your seatbelts. It's going to be a bumpy ride.

Begin with a Strong *Closing* Statement

When I prepare a case for trial, I always start at the end. Like a good mystery writer, I begin with my conclusion—then work backward, seeking ways to support that conclusion as convincingly as possible. This becomes my closing argument, which usually takes between twenty and forty-five minutes to deliver.

In a mystery, support for the detective's conclusion comes in the form of clues: a seemingly banal object that's suspiciously out of place; an odd off-handed remark by one of the suspects; a handwriting impression pulled from an otherwise blank note pad. In court, we rely on evidence that is as clear and unambiguous as possible: financial documents, contracts, bills of sale, medical records, police reports, and eye-witness testimony. Together, this evidence provides the foundation for the verdict we hope the judge will reach.

But before a judge can consider evidence, it must be accepted by the court. (This is when you hear a lawyer use the phrase "I wish to enter into evidence such-and-such.")

This is not as easy as it sounds. Opposing counsel can—and often *will*—object to an evidentiary submission by challenging either its authenticity or its relevance. A challenge to authenticity basically means you're saying the "thing," such as a document, may be fabricated. It may be a fake. (In this era of Photoshop and other computer-manipulated imagery, this is becoming an increasingly vexing problem.) Finally, a "challenge to relevance" simply means that while the item itself may be genuine and legitimate, it doesn't prove or disprove a legal element of the case.

Experience Counts

What makes the difference whether evidence is ultimately admitted or excluded from evidence? Sometimes it's the facts. But more often, it's the quality of the attorney. This is why you want a strong, experienced attorney on your side when you go to court. I know how to present evidence in a way judges will accept. And I know how to object to adversarial evidence in ways that undermines its credibility.

I always advise people looking for a divorce lawyer to limit their search to attorneys with a minimum five years of family law experience. It takes at least that long to develop the instincts necessary to become comfortable in the legal arena, to get to know all the local players, and to develop the skills to try a case successfully. Go with less-experienced lawyers and all you're doing is subsidizing their on-the-job training.

And *you* are the one who will pay for their mistakes. And, trust me, they *will* make mistakes.

In court, there are all kinds of ways for attorneys to trip up. It can be due to lack of preparation. Ignorance about the rules of evidence.

Not knowing about the hearsay rule exception. Not keeping their own facts straight. Not being unable to detect subtle lies (even from their own clients). Or simply not having the experience to see when the other side has handed you an opening.

You know how professional sports teams always watch film of an upcoming opponent's previous games to study their playing style, identify strengths, and target vulnerabilities? I'm the same way before going to trial. I've been in this game long enough I know just about all the other major players in the Orange County divorce scene, including the judges. I know how a certain lawyer is going to approach a certain kind of case. I can even sometimes predict how a specific judge will rule on a given motion. Armed with such knowledge, I can adjust my own presentation accordingly. I can target my adversaries' known weak spots and behave in ways likely to push their buttons.

Four words I love to hear in court are "I will move on." Especially when it comes from opposing counsel. Lawyers speak these words when, having objections against them sustained again and again, they simply abandon trying to submit a piece of evidence or pursue a line of questioning. It means they've given up. Surrendered. It means I've done my job. It means I'm winning.

Presentation Is Everything

I said it earlier, and I'll say it again: trials are won based not on the facts but on the lawyers. Yes, facts are important. But more important is how the facts are *presented*. To prevail, a case needs to be simple. It needs to be focused. It needs to be elegant. It's like the difference between trying to sell a luxury car using a ten-page sheet of engineering specifications versus a single, sexy picture and a catchy four-word slogan.

Trial

Simple wins every time.

It also helps to think of a trial as theater. If you ever serve on jury, you will inevitably be warned that a real trial is *not* like the courtroom dramas you see on TV or in the movies. And this is true, technically. For one thing, even the briefest of trials take a lot longer than two hours.

Yet you cannot discount the power of drama, emotion, and good old-fashioned storytelling in a courtroom trial. Like a good play, a legal presentation is well-structured, suspenseful, emotionally gripping, and expertly performed. It has heroes and villains.

It's also well-rehearsed. In the theater, an actor who continuously forgets lines, mumbles dialogue, and fails to connect with the other performers will be booed off the stage. Likewise, an attorney who's constantly searching for words, forgetting a line of questioning, or flailing in search of a point will lose credibility with the judge. Like a symphony conductor, a good attorney knows how to play each piece of the orchestra (in this case, the witnesses, the evidence, etc.), making sure each is heard at the right time for greatest impact.

A great lawyer knows how to put on a great show.

But while in the theater the literal truth is often bent and twisted for dramatic effect, in court an attorney must be *very* careful about the veracity of the facts one presents. The danger inherent in error—however small—is summed up in the old Latin phrase *falsus in uno falsus in omnibus*: "false in one thing, false in everything."

If you give the court reason to doubt you about *anything*, it can doubt you about *everything*. Which is why, when in court, I make it my mission to poke holes in as much of the opposition's evidence as I possibly can. (And, by the same token, ensure my own evidence is bulletproof.)

Control the Narrative

As covered earlier, a divorce is a civil litigation. But unlike the traditional lawsuit in which a plaintiff sues a defendant for relief from damages, such relief usually being in the form of money, here in no-fault California, there is no functional difference between petitioner (sometimes called the plaintiff) and respondent (sometimes called the defendant). Except for one thing: in court, the petitioner's side gets to speak first.

In court, speaking first is an advantage. *It allows you to set the stage.* Establish the parameters. It lets you control the narrative. Which is why I always prefer to represent a petitioner.

As the petitioner's attorney, I usually employ what is commonly known as the Abraham Lincoln Defense. This was a strategy famously used by the man who would become America's sixteenth president back when he was still practicing law in Illinois.

When advocating for a client, Lincoln would often begin by presenting the *opposition's* case, bringing up all the things the other side was likely to say about the party he represented, and then dismantling or dismissing those charges and accusations one by one. This way, when the opposition *did* try to make their case, not only had their accusations lost any shock value, but their charges had also already been refuted.

As a result, they look weak and floundering. More than a century-and-a-half later, this remains a potent and effective legal strategy.

Exploit Weakness

A courtroom is a jungle where any signs of weakness will be mercilessly exploited. In this sense, a good divorce lawyer is an apex predator who can quickly recognize vulnerabilities and go straight for the kill. Some classic signs of weakness I always look for in my opposition include the following.

Attorneys afraid of going to court. I have told you all the reasons *not* to go to court. But when a trial is my last, best option, I relish the opportunity. This is not true of all lawyers. Some truly *fear* going to court because of its unpredictability. When I sense this, I use it to my advantage. I make the threat of court so intense they have no choice but to roll over, giving us virtually everything we demand before we even make it up the courthouse steps.

Clients afraid of going to court. Sometimes it's the client, not the attorney, who's scared of court. They hate speaking in public. They detest the attention. They're terrified of being cross-examined. If I discover this, I know I can press for concessions I may not otherwise be able to get.

Lying. I love it when I'm up against a liar. And the more brazen, the better. Because nothing destroys a liar better or faster than the truth. If I can catch the opposition in a lie and produce evidence that proves it, their ass is mine. I can virtually dictate the terms of their surrender.

Uncertainty. You don't have to lie or even exaggerate to make yourself vulnerable. Simple hesitancy or uncertainty about a fact can be all I need to strike a mortal blow. This is why pretrial depositions are so valuable. When someone qualifies a response, equivocates, or is otherwise less than 100 percent confident in a response, I know this is a point I can attack in court.

In his 2005 book *Blink: The Power of Thinking without Thinking*, award-winning author Malcolm Gladwell explores how humans developed the ability to make snap judgments, to assess a potentially dangerous situation or size up a stranger in literally microseconds. Such intuition is one of the key reasons we, as humans, have been able to survive for millennia despite our many physical deficits compared to other animal species.[1] Experienced lawyers hone this ability to a fine edge, being able to assess a witness's veracity based on a brief conversation or a tell as subtle as a slight hesitation in a response.

Word choice is often a dead giveaway someone is hiding something. People who feel vulnerable choose their words *very* carefully. Often, unnaturally so. For example, in a deposition, if I ask a husband, "Did you ever hit your wife?" and his response is, "I never struck my wife in anger," I can sense something is up. The phrase "in anger" is not one uses in everyday conversation and is clearly cover for some other nefarious deed.

It's a thread I'm eager to pull.

The Different Judges You Might Encounter

Clients often ask me, what can I expect when I go to trial? My answer: that depends on the judge. There are basically two types.

The Straight Shooter. This judge looks at the law like a science, not an art. They know the rules and follow them explicitly. Like *Dragnet's* Sergeant Joe Friday, this judge is interested in "just the facts" and, like a trained scientist, follows the data to its logical conclusion. This judge is not impressed with theatrics or swayed by emotion. In court, it's best to stick with the program and avoid any side-trips or distractions.

The Omnivore. An omnivore eats anything. And like its biological namesake, this judge has a wide and virtually unlimited appetite for information. This judge doesn't like to hear objections to the admission of evidence. They want to know *everything*, even seemingly extraneous facts, so they can make the best possible decision.

If your judge is an omnivore, expect a long, perhaps even tedious trial. Passion and emotion are effective tools with this type. As an attorney, I like to play as much as I can off the judge's empathy. Neither type of judge is necessarily better than the other. But your attorney needs to know the judge's personality so strategy can be adjusted accordingly.

Taking the Stand

At some point in your divorce trial, you will be asked to take the witness stand and testify on your own behalf. The key to giving effective witness testimony is the same as responding effectively in a pretrial deposition: be brief, be concise, be specific, and *respond directly to the question asked*. Always remember, it is your lawyer's job to build your case, not yours. Follow your attorney's lead. Don't try to get ahead of them. Don't embellish. Don't exaggerate. Don't try to make points about things off-topic. Stay calm. Appear friendly. Remain confident.

It sounds easy, but for many people, it isn't. Courtroom testimony is the climax of what has probably been a years-long ordeal. Tension is high; emotions are at their peak; one's natural inclination is to explode with all the rage, resentment, bitterness, and vitriol that's been building steadily over time. Resist the urge. Even the subtlest loss of control during testimony—something as innocuous as a contemptuous snort or a dismissive eyeroll—may count against you.

Despite even the best preparation, it's not uncommon for witnesses to lose it on the stand. When it's my client who goes out of control, it's devastating to my case. When it's a witness for the other side who loses it, it's blood in the water. And it's delicious.

The following are some classic types of bad witnesses I've encountered during my many appearances in court.

The Juggernaut. This witness is always on the attack. No matter the question, the Juggernaut goes into full battle mode, hurling accusations, charges, and invectives like an out-of-control Terminator robot. But unlike a Terminator, the Juggernaut is not driven by cold, unfeeling algorithms, but by uncontrollable rage that burns with the heat of ten thousand suns. If this witness is my client, the best thing I can do is pull the plug as quickly as possible. If the Juggernaut is testifying for the other side, I just stand back and watch the show. The grave the Juggernaut digs is always its own.

The Know-It-All. The Know-It-All is usually a narcissist determined to prove they're the smartest person in the room. Every response turns into a lecture designed to demonstrate their intellectual superiority. Of course, the irony here is that, more often than not, the Know-It-All doesn't know what the hell they're talking about, and their obvious BSing only undermines their credibility. When I have a Know-It-All on the stand, I control the response by asking very specific questions and then cutting them off when I have the answer I need. If the Know-It-All is testifying for the opposition, I usually begin by flattering their so-called expertise and then quickly pick up on inconsistencies, embellishments, and contradictions in their testimony. It's actually kind of fun.

The Compulsive Liar. The Compulsive Liar has no regard for the truth and simply says whatever they believe supports their position at any particular moment. This type of witness is potentially very dangerous because they believe what they say at the time they say it, even though they may totally contradict themselves just a few minutes later. Such utter confidence can be quite persuasive, and it takes a skilled attorney armed with unassailable evidence to break them on the witness stand.

The Blabbermouth. This witness usually takes the stand visibly nervous. Their hands tremble when they take their oath. There's often sweat on their forehead and/or upper lip. They try to deal with their anxiety by talking incessantly. Even when asked a simple yes or no question, they respond with paragraphs of explanations, clarifications, and qualifications. They try to curry favor with the attorneys by anticipating lines of questioning and responding to queries that have not even be posed. The Blabbermouth inevitably says something stupid or self-incriminating, which is why my advice for such individuals is always the same: *Just. Shut. Up.*

Often, one of these witness types ends up speaking in trial. Which is why witness preparation is so important. Before a deposition, and especially before a trial, I insist on working with each witness to polish their presentation and fine-tune their testimony. Of course, they must always tell the truth, but only the specific truth requested of them. Nothing less, and certainly nothing more.

The right preparation can turn a bad witness into a great one.

When you take the witness stand, your lawyer will be the one who will do the asking. You will sit in a wooden chair on a small dais to the judge's left. You will be asked to raise your right hand and swear to tell the truth. And then I will have you tell your story via a series of very specific questions.

When you respond, be sure to do so directly to the question your lawyer has asked. If the question requires a yes or no answer, simply reply yes or no. Don't go beyond that. Don't *explain* why you responded the way you did unless your lawyer specifically *asks* you to do so. Try to keep all your answers short, sweet, and to the point. Keep as much *negative* emotion out of your voice as possible. (*Positive* emotion, on the other hand, always works to your benefit.)

When your attorney is done, your spouse's attorney will then conduct cross-examination. The intent here will be to undermine or otherwise cast doubt on your original testimony, to catch you in a lie or, at the very least, an inconsistency. This is the time to be very, very careful. If you don't understand a question, say so and ask that it be repeated. Take your time before responding. Also, try to keep all answers well timed and evenly spaced.

Again, keep your answers brief and to the point.

During cross-examination, you are likely to hear your attorney object to one or more of the opposing counsel's questions. *What is an objection?* Technically, it is a protest based on the contention that the question or evidence is improper, inadmissible, or otherwise contrary to the court's rules of evidence.

Or, in the words of comedian Jerry Seinfeld, "'Objection' is the adult version of "fraid not!' To which the judge can say two things. He can say 'overruled,' which is the adult version of "fraid so!' Or he can say, 'sustained,' which is the adult version of 'duh!'"[2]

If you hear your lawyer object, stop talking. They will give the judge their reason for the objection, after which the judge will rule on its validity. If the judge sustains their objection, the lawyer questioning you will either rephrase the question or ask a different one. If the judge overrules their objection, then you will have to answer the question as it was originally posed. If, at this point, you don't remember the exact question, you can ask the attorney to repeat it. If nothing else, use the interruption to carefully consider your response.

The Yellow Pad Solution

During your divorce trial, you will be judged during every moment you spend in the courtroom. This means not just the brief time you'll have on the witness stand, but the many hours you will spend sitting at either the petitioner or respondent's table watching the lawyers make their case. Sitting doing nothing can be exhausting, and few people are up to the task.

As witness after witness takes the stand, you will squirm, you will fidget, and you will *react* to the testimony via body language, facial expressions, sometimes even verbally. Such reactions can seriously influence your case. Every snort, grimace, balled fist, and eyeroll you make will be seen by the judge and used to construct a mental picture of your character. Probably to your detriment.

A tool I use to effectively mitigate this problem is the simple legal-sized yellow pad. Before testimony begins, I provide my clients with a pad and pen and instruct them to write down their reactions to the testimony they hear, including points they believe I need to challenge, and questions they would like me to ask the various witnesses. This not only gives clients something to do with their hands but also provides a way to channel their anger, frustration, and other negative emotions in a manner less likely to upset the judge. It also supplies me ammunition I can use (or choose not to use) in cross-examination.

The Case of the Witless Witness

Dean and Carly had built a huge marketing empire that included videos, social media, and SEO. They were multimillionaires, but their incessant bickering ultimately led to the collapse of what had once been a $40 million operation.

During their divorce trial, Carly was unable to control her rage. At the slightest provocation, she would rant and rave about how Dean had undermined her authority during meetings, mismanaged employees, and misappropriated as much as $10 million in company funds. Even her own attorney was unable to get her to moderate her attacks. It was clear that this constant stream of vitriol was getting on the judge's nerves.

When it was Dean's turn to present his case, his lawyer not only produced multiple witnesses who contradicted Carly's description of her husband's professional behavior but also submitted forensic evidence that Dean had *not*, in fact, misappropriated the funds as per his wife's accusations. In sharp contrast to Carly's presentation, Dean's was terse, unemotional, and backed by solid evidence. Faced with such evidence, Carly was forced under cross-examination to recant many of her previous charges.

Not surprisingly, the judge decided to "charge" Carly for her misbehavior by awarding Dean much of the remaining cash the pair would have otherwise split. Carly literally paid for her misconduct.

The moral of the story: while courtrooms are great settings for drama, the person who pays for literal courtroom theatrics may be *you*.

The Ruling

At the conclusion of your trial, after you and your spouse have testified, after supporting witnesses have been questioned and cross-examined, after evidence has been submitted by both parties, the judge will make their ruling. This will cover all aspects of your divorce that have not already been settled, which can include:

- Determination of separate and community property

- Division of community property

- How jointly owned property (like homes, vehicles, etc.) will be awarded

- How business interests will be valued and/or divided

- Who owes who

- Details of spousal support and child support

- Custody arrangements and visitation schedules for minor children

All these details will then be documented in a divorce decree or judgment. The final document you will receive from the court is a notice of entry of judgment. (This is equivalent to a death certificate officially verifying someone is, in fact, dead.) And if you now want to marry someone else—*don't*! I'm kidding. But seriously, wait for this document before you start the nuptials. Or you may be getting into bigamous territory!

At this point, congratulations, you are now legally, officially, and formally divorced. But that's not the end of the story. A divorce may be the end of the marriage, but it's not the end of the tale. And if kids are involved, it's definitely not the end of your relationship. You still have quite a bit of work ahead of you.

Read on!

10

POSTDIVORCE

Your divorce is now final. Congratulations. (Or condolences, depending on your current state of mind.) Like a wedding, a graduation, or having your first child, a divorce is a major life milestone. For better or worse, things will never be the same.

But just because your divorce is final doesn't mean your work is done. Far from it. During your marriage, you constructed a matrix of legal, financial, and identity networks that now must be systematically dismantled and rebuilt. Depending on the length and complexity of your marriage, rebooting your life can take months, even years.

Your divorce decree will contain more than just a legal certification that your marriage has ended. It will also detail all the rights and obligations you have assumed under the decree, many of which require timely action. Read the decree carefully to understand exactly what is required of you. Things to look for are:

- Actions you must take and the deadlines and potential penalties involved

- Titles that need to be transferred from joint form to individual

- Deeds that need to be drafted and recorded

- QDROs (Qualified Domestic Relations Orders) that have to be completed on certain retirement assets

- Beneficiaries of life insurance policies designed to secure certain obligations that need to be confirmed

- Remaining joint accounts (e.g., checking, savings) that must be closed to prevent further use

- Health insurance changes that are needed

Many of these changes can be anticipated well in advance of the actual decree, so you should start preparing ahead of time. For example, contact your bank to close any joint accounts and reestablish new ones in your own names. You'll also need new checks with your name and address. (Note: The judgment will divide any remaining joint accounts, such as IRAs, 401(k)s, etc.)

Other things you can do in advance include the following:

- Contact your credit card companies and lenders to remove your name from any accounts/debts for which you are no longer responsible. You should also open at least one new account to establish credit in your own name if you don't have one already.

- Change the passwords on all your online accounts and memberships.

- If you're reverting to your maiden name, make sure all your financial accounts, insurance, and any other accounts and documents reflect this. This includes getting a new driver's license, notifying Social Security of your name change, and alerting all the financial and investment institutions with which you do business.

- Prepare to change the titles on your motor vehicles to reflect the new ownership status.

- Likewise, contact your auto insurance company to get ready to change details on owners, addresses, and so on.

- Write a new will (if you have not already done so). Note: California probate code sections 6122 and 6122.1 detail the automatic revocation of any disposition of property to a former spouse or domestic partner.

- Create a new estate plan.

- If you were on a joint family health insurance plan, get one in your own name or remove your spouse as the plan's rules may dictate.

- Contact your accountant to discuss the impending changes in your tax status.

Other Life Changes

The preceding checklist covers the one-time steps you need to take to establish your new, single life. But there are other changes you must implement that reflect your new long-term/recurring obligations and responsibilities. These include the following:

- Budget for monthly spousal and/or child support as directed by your divorce decree.

- Make sure you actually *pay* the monthly support as ordered. Keep records of all payments as there is no statute of limitations on missed payments.

- Create a household budget reflecting your new postdivorce status.

- Schedule for co-parenting or visitation times as per the divorce decree. Likely you have been doing this already. I recommend keeping to the judgment, being flexible, and keeping a record.

The Case of the Deadbeat Corpse

After fifteen years of marriage, Leonard and Phyllis decided to call it quits. As part of the divorce decree, the judge ruled that Leonard should pay Phyllis $1,000 a month in child support to care for their then-five-year-old son. Leonard, being a responsible father, paid as ordered promptly on the first of each month.

However, in the fourth year of the divorce, Leonard was tragically killed by a drunk driver who ran a red light and T-boned his car while driving through an intersection at 11:00 at night. During the probate process, Phyllis sued Leonard's estate for what she claimed was four years of unpaid child-support. Yes, Phyllis was claiming Leonard had been a deadbeat father.

As Leonard's lawyer, it was my obligation to prove that he had, in fact, made his child support payments. The problem was that Leonard was a lousy record-keeper and there was no direct evidence he had met his court-mandated obligations. Even the bank records were inconclusive. In the end, I was able to convince Phyllis to accept less than the amount she had sued for, but no payment would have been necessary at all had Leonard been more meticulous with his record-keeping while still among the living.

A Clean Break?

Hopefully, the details of your divorce represent a clean break from your ex-spouse. Although a divorce is, by definition, a severing of marital ties, many—*too* many, I would argue—people think they can and even *should* maintain some kind of formal relationship with their ex even after they have legally split. I am not talking about joint custody or co-parenting arrangements, which I fully support and encourage.

No, I'm talking about maintaining joint ownership in a business, continuing to co-own property, or even co-owning a home. These kinds of arrangements can last years or even decades. And following a divorce, they can be a source of major headaches. There are instances where this has worked. But there are arguably more where they do not.

In the event of divorce, I always advise my clients to break from their ex as completely and as cleanly as possible where business and financial matters are concerned. It's nearly impossible to separate professional from personal interests, and fallout from your split will inevitably spill over into any working relationship you hope to maintain. Remember, there's a reason you got divorced in the first place: *You no longer get along!* For the sake of your company and your *employees*, cut the cord.

No business benefits from postdivorce personal drama.

Appellate Process

What happens if the judge hands down what you consider to be a bad decision? What if you find the judge's terms legally or factually wrong? What are your options?

Request for a Statement of Decision

At the end of a divorce trial, the judge will announce their decision on how the divorce should be finalized. This is usually done orally from the bench. Note that this ruling is not final but only a tentative decision that is subject to revision. If everyone is satisfied with the ruling, nothing needs to be done. In ten days, it will automatically become final, its elements locked in place.

However, if you are *not* happy with the ruling, you can ask your lawyer to submit a request for a statement of decision, which is a request for a written explanation of how the judge arrived at their decision. Both parties—you and your ex—have ten days to make such a request.

If you are on the losing side of the case, the statement of decision process—and I do mean *process*—is necessary to do the following:

- *Attempt to change the judge's initial tentative ruling.* The request asks the court to explain its reasoning on the principal controverted issues by setting forth their factual and legal basis for the tentative decision.

- *Set the foundation for an appeal.* The court's response will determine whether its rulings are supported by the facts and the law.

- *Give the appellate court the means to overturn the ruling.* The statement of decision is likely the first thing the appellate court will review in an appeal. Without one, the appellate court will presume the lower court had the necessary findings of fact to support its decision.

Raise Objections to the Statement of Decision and Judgment

Once the court has issued its proposed judgment and statement decision, either party, meaning either you or your ex, may file objections to its content. There is no specific format required for this, but it must adequately object to the decision based on the *facts* and the *law* as they apply to your case. Both these steps are essential if you are going to appeal the divorce court's ruling. Failing to do either will result in a waiver to your right of appeal.

Postdivorce Legal Issues

Just because your divorce is final doesn't *necessarily* mean your legal woes are over. Even if your divorce was not particularly contentious, there's no guarantee your spouse will abide by all the orders contained in your divorce decree. And even with the best of intentions, changing circumstances may prompt you or your ex to seek changes in your original divorce settlement. Should issues arise, you may yet again find yourself talking to your lawyer.

Common postdivorce issues that may require a legal remedy include the following.

Enforcement of orders. It's not uncommon for an ex to fail to fully execute all aspects of a divorce decree, fall behind on spousal or child support, or otherwise fail to fulfill all postdivorce obligations. In this case, you can seek a contempt citation from the court to force compliance.

Modification of custody orders. As a result of changing circumstances, you may seek to change the custody and/or visitation particulars of your divorce settlement. Factors that can warrant such a change include you or your spouse moving to a new city, state, or country; changes in work schedules; a strong preference of a child to live with one parent over another; or proof of irresponsible parenting by one's former spouse.

Changes to spousal or child support. There are situations when one party's financial circumstances change significantly for the better—or for the worse—warranting a change in how spousal and/or child support is arranged. For example, the individual charged with paying support may lose a job and no longer be able to pay as originally ordered, or the individual who is receiving support may experience a cash windfall and no longer need it.

Embrace Your New Life

No matter how well you think you are prepared for your new life post-divorce, seeing the actual decree in black and white will likely be a shock. Even if you and your ex have been living apart for months—or even years—prior to receiving the final decree, you will likely experience a flood of conflicting emotions: joy, sorrow, relief, fear, elation, and guilt. You may wish to seek professional counseling or join a divorce support group. You should certainly consult with a financial adviser to create a plan that will provide the financial stability you need during this difficult time.

Therapists will tell you that this is the time to embrace your new life. To reassess your priorities and start building anew. My advice, as a lawyer, is to take things slowly. Don't make any major lifestyle changes or embark on any risky undertakings for at least a year. Sure, take that long-overdue vacation. Buy a new outfit. Try a new hobby. But maybe that $100,000 sports car can wait a while. For now, just *breathe*. Enjoy the peace and quiet.

Until the kids start screaming . . .

Maybe give it a year or two before you jump back into the institution known as marriage. And when you do—please get a prenuptial agreement.

Let's Hear from the Experts

In this, the final section of the book, I will turn things over to some experts in the field for their thoughts on various aspects of the divorce process. It's my hope that these interviews help you along in your divorce journey.

How to Bounce Back from Divorce:
A Life Coach's Advice

Anita Kanti, a.k.a. Anita K, is a professional life coach who has been practicing in Orange County, California, for years. A divorcee herself, she has been featured by *Good Day LA*, *Better Homes and Gardens*, Fox 11 Los Angeles, *Huffpost*, and *Axios*. Trained and certified by Tony Robbins's Robbins-Madanes program, she's counseled dozens of clients on how to grow and thrive postdivorce.

Q: What went wrong with your own marriage?

A: I met the man who would become my husband when I was in high school. We came from similar backgrounds, cut from the same cloth. Same culture. Same pressures. We had both been raised in traditional Indian American households, and we both bought into the old-fashioned American dream. This meant the house in the suburbs, a white picket fence, two kids, a good job—preferably in corporate America—and so on.

So marriage just seemed like the logical step. Yet we didn't rush into things. In fact, we didn't marry until I was twenty-five. And I thought it would work. He was my best friend, but over time things began to unravel organically.

Q: How so?

A: Looking back, I think my husband really didn't want to be married. He did it because it was *expected* of him. And he married me because he saw me as a good mother for his children. But as far as being a husband—the responsibility, the monogamy—he really wasn't ready for that. As he grew, he discovered things about himself that didn't fit into the normal all-American life. This tension manifested in stress, which he kept bottled up for years. We started having communication breakdowns. And because we really didn't understand ourselves—we lacked the maturity and confidence to talk through our problems—things progressively worsened. He sank into alcoholism, and later was diagnosed as bipolar. After ten years, I finally walked away from the marriage. We had one daughter at the time, and we did not (originally) part on good terms. We were constantly fighting. Back then, I didn't have the skills to understand how to deal with someone who was battling dual illnesses.

Q: What turned things around?

A: Before we separated, he had started going to AA meetings. He came home one day with a pamphlet for Al-Anon. He said, "My sponsor thinks this might help you." I was very offended. *I* wasn't the one with the problem; *he* was. But I read the pamphlet and, after two or three weeks, decided to check it out, not really knowing what to expect. And it really helped! I learned that this wasn't all about *me*. I could separate my needs and my pain and understand the illness behind what my husband was battling. And I think that kind of catapulted me into getting interested in learning more about how to heal myself, staying in my lane and not really getting into his, and trying to understand myself, how far I've come, and what all this means.

Q: How long were you and your husband separated before you divorced?

A: Three years. We wanted to see if we could get together after that, but we couldn't. The divorce ended peacefully, but it was still very sad, and he didn't really welcome it. He didn't want it, but he was very cooperative. And then I started the process of healing, and I became a life coach rather by accident. I have a background of over fifteen years in corporate talent acquisition and HR where coaching is done very organically. When I started going through programs, books, seminars, therapy, yoga sessions—even flying to India to learn meditation—is when I realized there is something to all this.

Q: And that's when you went through the Robbins-Madanes program.

A: Yes. I think Tony Robbins is terrific. He knows how to help people become their best selves.

Q: As a life coach and someone who has experienced divorce herself, what is your advice for someone leaving a marriage?

A: First and foremost, you must understand and accept where you are. Claim your feelings. Trust your emotional experience. There is no right way or wrong way to feel about what you're going through. The emotions you're feeling are yours and yours alone. Accept them as valid. Next, you have to talk it out with the help of a *team*. And you must pick this team very carefully. It's natural to immediately turn to a parent, a sibling, or a best friend, but this is often a mistake. Unless they, too, have been divorced, they won't be able to truly understand and empathize with what you're experiencing. Friends and family members are also apt to be judgmental, even if they don't mean to be, and that's the last thing you need right now. Instead, I suggest going to a support group with other recent divorcees. Also, seeking the services of a professional, licensed therapist can be extremely useful. Keep the circle small. Maybe two or three people, tops.

Q: What else?

A: Getting your finances in order is a top priority. You need to get an immediate handle on your budget, your monthly income, expenses, rent, other obligations, and so on. If you don't get your money affairs in order quickly, your whole life can fall apart really, really fast.

Q: You've emphasized the need for keeping communication lines open with your ex. Why?

A: This is absolutely critical if there's a child involved. Your ex has to remain part of the picture. And, trust me, I know how difficult this can be, especially when the divorce is fresh. Emotions are high. You're dealing with feelings of betrayal and abandonment. But you have to step back and be as *businesslike* as possible. I know a lot of couples can't do this. There's too much anger. But if you and your ex can't get along in a civilized fashion, it's the kids who are going to suffer the most.

Q: What's your advice about dealing with all the negativity people feel when divorcing?

A: This is where self-care comes in. You must make your mental and emotional health a top priority. This can mean seeking counseling from a therapist or priest. Going to a yoga retreat. Working with a nutritionist. Making sure you eat right, get enough sleep, and exercise. Prioritizing self-care is absolutely key because it's one of the few things you have control over, and maintaining your physical, mental, and emotional health will help ease the pain you are experiencing. (And it's a lot better for you than junk food, alcohol, and smoking.)

Q: So far, you've talked a lot about self-care. What about care of others?

A: Self-care naturally comes first. It's like when you're on an airplane and the flight attendant tells you that in the event of an emergency put your own oxygen mask on first before you help your kids. The same thing applies here. If you don't take care of yourself, you won't be in any shape to help anyone else. But once you get that established then, yes, your children's needs come next. Check in with them regularly to see how they're feeling. And never press them to take sides. Children should never be used as pawns; nor should they be asked to favor one parent over another.

Q: As painful as divorce is, can it also be an opportunity?

A: Any trauma that shatters complacency is an opportunity for self-reevaluation. You know how the COVID lockdowns caused millions of people to reassess what they wanted to do with their lives? In just a few months, many people changed jobs, shifted careers, and embarked on whole new life paths. Divorce offers the same challenges and opportunities. Your old life has been stripped away and now you can rebuild it in a way that may be better, more fulfilling.

Q: How long does recovering from a divorce usually take?

A: Expect it to take at least a year. For me, personally, it was two years. But trust the process. It *will* happen. It may not seem that way when you're in the middle of it, but, trust me, you *will* get through it.

Q: Is there anything one can do to speed up the process?

A: Forgiveness can help remove the toxic atmosphere you're living in. Now, you might say, "How can I forgive my ex? He cheated on me twelve times. That's unforgiveable." And, from a moral perspective, that may be true. But holding that resentment isn't going to help you move on. Once you can stop making everything about *you*—when you come to understand that cheating was the result of a weakness and failure in your spouse's character—then you can find the strength to move on.

Q: What else can help divorcees move on?

A: I'm a big fan of vision boards. Every year, I put together a board filled with pictures that help me visualize the experiences I hope to have and the life I wish to live in the year ahead. It's a tool I use to focus my mind on the goals I hope to achieve. And this can include entering new relationships, finding a new love. A divorce may be the end of a marriage, but it's not the end of your story. You have the whole rest of your life to live. Learn from your experience and use those lessons to move toward the future you want.

Postdivorce

Headed for Divorce? You Can Learn from a Forensic Expert

Denis Retoske is a triple-threat: an attorney, a certified public accountant (CPA), and a certified valuation analyst (CVA). He often serves as a forensic accountant in divorces, analyzing documents to help family court judges decide on child and spousal support payments, as well as how to divide community property. Denis holds memberships in the American Institute of Certified Public Accountants (AICPA), the AICPA's Forensic Valuation Services section, and the National Association of Certified Valuators and Analysts. More than three decades of being a CPA, and nearly two decades of forensic accounting experience, afford Denis particular insight into how to obtain the best outcome in a divorce.

Q: What steps do you take to determine recommendations for property division and spousal support?

A: Generally, the first issue to be addressed in divorce is to analyze the income of the parties. I review a couple's household and business activities to determine how much income—how much cash flow—is available to pay temporary spousal support and, if there are minor children, child support.

The income analysis is done to determine *temporary* support, the support needed to maintain the status quo during the pendency of the litigation, which can take several months or even years.

The income analysis is almost always required to be updated to help determine *permanent* spousal support, the goal of which is to allow the recipient spouse to become self-supporting in a reasonable time. It's thus normally lower than temporary support. Permanent support can only be modified in the case of death or remarriage of the supported spouse, death of the payor spouse, or by further order of the court. Keep in mind, the respective income of the parties is one of *many* financial and nonfinancial factors courts must consider in determining *permanent* spousal support. So temporary support and permanent support are designed to serve different purposes.

Q: So, what is a marital balance sheet?

A: A marital balance sheet shows all the assets and liabilities of a marital estate that are to be characterized, valued, and divided such as real estate, investment accounts, retirement accounts, business interests, jewelry, art, mortgages, and other liabilities. The net worth of the parties is also a factor the court considers in determining permanent spousal support.

When one party in a dissolution proceeding continues to pay certain community debts—for example, real estate taxes or a mortgage—with post-separation earnings, that person is likely entitled reimbursements, which are also shown on the marital balance sheet. When testifying in a trial or hearing, I often testify to the current income of one or both the parties, the net worth of the parties, and the marital standard of living. (This is often referred to as the station in life the parties achieved during marriage.)

Q: What advice would you give to an entrepreneur/business owner getting married or contemplating divorce to ensure the best possible outcome?

A: Regardless of whether there is a prenuptial agreement or subsequent transmutation (the change of separate property to community property or community property to separate property), I recommend keeping detailed records of all financial transactions—including the purchase of assets from the start of the marriage, and better yet, *prior* to the marriage. (This helps characterize all property at the date of marriage and afterward.) I also recommend keeping them *forever*, year by year, month by month. Banks and other financial institutions generally only retain records for seven years. You can't count on them to provide the records later if you get divorced. Possessing detailed records going back to the start of a marriage and before can potentially save tens of thousands of dollars in legal and accounting fees.

Next, if you have received or expect to receive an inheritance or gift you wish to keep separate from your community property, put it in a separate account and keep it separate to avoid commingling separate and community funds. This way it is simpler to tell what separate property was prior to the marriage or received during the marriage.

Finally, you must realize emotion often drives a divorce. This can make the case harder and pricier than it needs to be, especially in straightforward divorces. It is important to be honest and make full disclosures. If you reach an amicable agreement with your soon to be ex-spouse, I often recommend having a family law attorney review the agreement to ensure both parties have addressed their rights and obligations.

Ultimately, there's no substitute for good counsel in a divorce. Family can be complex, and an experienced lawyer can help navigate the trickiest situations.

Planning for Your Financial Success— despite Divorce

Wealth manager Loreen Gilbert, CEO and founder of WealthWise Financial Services has spent more than three decades creating comprehensive wealth strategies for clients spanning twenty-six states. In 2021, she made both the *Forbes* Top Female Advisor list and the *Forbes* Best-in-State Wealth Advisors. Recognized by the ThinkAdvisor Luminaries Class of 2021 in the Thought Leadership category, for nine consecutive years, Loreen received the Five Star Wealth Manager Award.

A proactive financial strategist, Loreen has worked extensively with high earners—men and women—who are contemplating or are in the midst of a divorce. This experience helped her develop critical strategies to aid individuals weather the financial shocks that inevitably come with a marital dissolution, regardless of income status. Loreen has been profiled and quoted by CNBC, *Bloomberg*, Fox, TD Ameritrade, *Cheddar*, *US News and World Report*, *USA Today*, *Yahoo! Finance*, Reuters, *Plan Sponsor Magazine*, and *WealthManagement*. Currently, she hosts the *WealthWise Moment*, an on-air segment for KX FM and an iTunes podcast. As the author of a soon-to-be-released book, *WealthWise for Women: Your Vision, Your Values, Your Financial Independence*, Loreen has a passion for educating women on the topic of financial empowerment.

Loreen is a registered representative with LPL Financial, a registered investment advisor and member of FINRA/SIPC.

Q: Why is wealth planning before a divorce so critical?

A: If you're contemplating divorce, try to assess what your financial situation will look like when you're without your spouse. You must consider not only what your income will likely be but also your *obligations*. For example, if you have children who are likely to go to college, who will pay for their higher education? If they are currently in private school, who will pay for *what*? Do your children participate in club sports?

Those can be expensive. Who will cover the costs? Do you expect to be responsible for child support? Alimony? If so, how is that likely to affect your future lifestyle? Also, if you expect to receive alimony and/or child support, will it be enough to cover your monthly expenses? If not, how will you make up the shortfall?

Keep in mind when determining monthly expenses, you can't just take what you're spending now as a couple, divide the number in half, and figure that's what you'll need to maintain your current living standard. There are many economies of scale associated with being a couple that vanish when single. Once divorced, you'll need to have your own house, condo, or apartment. You'll also be paying for your own utilities, not to mention, your own grocery, phone, internet, and streaming service bills. You'll be saving for your own retirement, too. These considerations probably won't stop you from getting the divorce you seek, but they should affect the particulars of the settlement you pursue.

Q: When's the best time to make these essential determinations, especially those that will affect your children?

A: These are not questions you can answer by yourself. They are issues you must discuss with your (outgoing) spouse. So the earliest you can broach these topics is once divorce proceedings are underway. The mistake many people make is waiting until the divorce is *finalized* to talk about seemingly banal issues like paying for kids' back-to-school clothing, college, weddings, and so on.

The feeling is that these questions will just muddy the waters during what may already be contentious negotiations regarding major issues, such as custody. But the postdivorce period can be just as combative. So I always encourage my clients to address these issues as soon as possible, before the settlement has a chance to be written in stone, as it were. Always approach these topics sooner, not later.

Q: What can people do to get their finances in order before divorce?

A: The first thing to do is get a good family law attorney. This usually means an *expensive* attorney. You'll have to put money aside just for your legal representation. Ensure you have enough to pay your lawyer *and* cover your day-to-day household expenses. Next, make sure any separate property is put into a separate trust. (By separate property, I mean any real estate you brought into the marriage or any inheritance you received before or during the marriage.) These must be separate accounts so that in the event of divorce you can easily prove they are yours and yours alone.

Ideally, any marriage should consider having three trust accounts, one for each spouse, and one for joint assets. After that, once a divorce is underway, you will want to meet with a financial advisor to establish your long-term financial goals, determine what amount of house you'll be able to afford, how you need to save for retirement, and how to ensure you won't run out of money.

What I often see is that one spouse receives a big divorce settlement and then becomes paralyzed because they don't know what to do with it, especially if they were the out-spouse. This is why it's critical to work with a financial advisor. Unfortunately, during a divorce, emotions tend to run so high that people invest all their emotional energy in the fight at hand rather than also planning for their future.

Q: What do you mean by "out-spouse"?

A: In many marriages, only one spouse is responsible for handling most or even all the financial matters. It can be the husband, or it can be the wife. We call the person who has the knowledge of the assets, and therefore the power in the relationship, the "in-spouse." The other person is the "out-spouse." Out-spouses are invariably at a disadvantage because they don't have a strong handle on the family's assets or debts and/or are uncomfortable handling large monetary decisions.

Q: Can a financial advisor work in tandem with a divorce attorney?

A: Not only *can* they; they *should*. Divorce attorneys understand the law, but they don't always appreciate the complexities of the financial issues at stake. For example, I had a client come to me at the end of his divorce proceedings—it would have been better at the beginning—with questions involving a complex deferred compensation plan he had with his employer. If he had involved me earlier, we probably could have worked everything out with the opposing counsel. But now, this late in the game, it's turned into a million-dollar problem we are *still* trying to resolve. Whether it's deferred compensation plans, 401(k)s, pension plans, or business ownership interests, all these assets must be approached carefully, recognizing the specific tax implications. A financial planner who understands the retirement plan and business ownership landscape can assist early during divorce proceedings to help avoid unintended consequences.

Q: What else should those contemplating divorce need to prepare for?

A: Surprisingly, most people aren't ready for the psychological, emotional, and financial adjustments required when they're suddenly on their own. Divorce can mean a major lifestyle change. This can take months, sometimes years, in which to get accustomed. Here's an example: Because of the divorce, you may have sold a home and bought a new one. If so, you might be in a new neighborhood and may be dealing with less space. All your old habits and previous assumptions need to be updated or rethought in the very least. Also, if you're paying alimony, you now have less disposable income. And if you're receiving alimony, you must deal with the fact that those payments may not last forever.

Q: Even if lifetime alimony is specified in the divorce decree?

A: Yes. I just went through this issue with one of my clients. She was to receive alimony in perpetuity, or until she remarried. A few years after the divorce, her ex-husband went to court and asked that the terms be changed, even though he was making more money than when they had divorced. To my client's surprise, the judge granted his request. Bottom line: take nothing for granted. Even if it's on paper in the divorce decree.

Q: What are other common mistakes people make when getting divorced?

A: They go into a divorce with the assumption that they will get everything they want. They don't understand that divorce is a *negotiation*. You must go into the proceedings with two lists: "must-haves" and "nice-to-haves." The must-haves are your nonnegotiables. They are the battles you need to win. The nice-to-haves are your bargaining chips. If you get them, great. If not, you can move on with your life. You want to have a big, healthy list of nice-to-haves so you possess options, items you can give up to secure your must-haves.

Q: Once the divorce decree is final, what's the first thing one should do?

A: Once the decree is final and you know exactly what the settlement terms are, it's time to sit down with your financial advisor to perform a thorough cash flow analysis. Together, you must determine exactly how much money you have, how to allocate those resources, and how long it will last.

Q: Even if you've received a large settlement?

A: Absolutely. If you've received, say, a five-million-dollar settlement—which to many people sounds like a lot of money—you can easily blow through it in just a few years, especially if you came from a high-income, high-net-worth household. (People who make a lot of money tend to *spend* a lot of money, and that's where the recently divorced can get into trouble.) If you're a spouse who didn't work, you may have to *go* to work to maintain the comfort level you desire.

Q: Do you have any advice specifically for men or for women?

A: Because many wives insist on getting the house, they can end up living in a place they can no longer afford. They become "house poor," having to maintain a home with property taxes and upkeep costs that are beyond their financial means. There are times when I advise my female clients to sell the residence they won in their divorce and use the proceeds to buy a smaller, more affordable place more in line with their current income and asset situation.

Q: Any final thoughts, especially on how to avoid being financially blindsided by a divorce?

A: Know where the money is. Even if you're the out-spouse. A few years ago, someone I knew went through a messy divorce that involved a *lot* of assets. The wife had let her husband handle all the finances for years and only had a vague idea of their net worth. When they began divorce proceedings, their net worth turned out to be far less than she thought. The husband claimed the money had all been spent during the marriage. It later turned out he had quietly moved most of it offshore over the years. At the end of the day, the wife lost millions.

Don't let this happen to you. Know where the money is and what assets there are. It's yours, and you have every right to it.

NOTES

Foreword

1. Laurie Yarnell, "Even with Maturity and Experience, Second Marriages Are Even More Likely to End in Divorce than First Ones," *Good Housekeeping*, January 31, 2023, https://www.goodhousekeeping.com/life/relationships/a42638493/second-marriages-divorce/.

Introduction

1. Anna Miller, "Can This Marriage Be Saved?," *Monitor on Psychology*, April 2013, https://www.apa.org/monitor/2013/04/marriage.

2. Nicholas H. Wolfinger, "Want to Avoid Divorce? Wait to Get Married, but Not Too Long," Institute for Family Studies, July 16, 2015, https://ifstudies.org/blog/want-to-avoid-divorce-wait-to-get-married-but-not-too-long/.

3. Nathan Yau, "Divorce Rates and Income," FlowingData, May 4, 2021, https://flowingdata.com/2021/05/04/divorce-rates-and-income/.

4. World Population Review, "Divorce Rate by State," January 2023, https://worldpopulationreview.com/state-rankings/divorce-rate-by-state.

5. World Population Review, "Divorce Rate by State."

6. Casey E. Copen, Kimberly Daniels, Jonathan Vespa, and William D. Mosher, "First Marriages in the United States: Data from the 2006–2010 National Survey of Family Growth," *National Health Statistics Reports*, no. 49 (March 22, 2012), https://www.cdc.gov/nchs/data/nhsr/nhsr049.pdf.

Chapter 1

1. "The Origins of Marriage," *The Week*, January 8, 2015, https://theweek.com/articles/528746/origins-marriage.

2. Kathleen Manning, "What Is the History of Marriage?," *U.S. Catholic*, October 9, 2012, https://uscatholic.org/articles/201210/what-is-the-history-of-marriage/.

3. Ruhi Nayak, "Harmful Representation: Arranged Marriage in Netflix's 'Indian Matchmaking,'" *Harvard Political Review*, December 11, 2022, https://harvardpolitics.com/harmful-representation-arranged-marriage-in-netflixs-indian-matchmaking/; Harriet Sherwood, "The Jewish Matchmaker," *The Guardian*, January 7, 2011, https://www.theguardian.com/lifeandstyle/2011/jan/07/jewish-matchmaker-arranged-marriage.

4. Leo Tolstoy, *The Complete Works of Lyof N. Tolstoi*, vol. 1, *Anna Karenina* (New York: Thomas Y. Crowell, 1899), 1.

5. California Online Divorce Assistance Service, "How Much Is an Uncontested Divorce in California?," accessed May 1, 2023, https://www.californiaonlinedivorce.com/how-much-is-an-uncontested-divorce-in-california/.

6. Darlena Cunha, "The Divorce Gap," *The Atlantic*, April 28, 2016, https://www.theatlantic.com/business/archive/2016/04/the-divorce-gap/480333/.

7. Ben Steverman, "Divorce Destroys Finances of Americans over 50, Studies Show," *Bloomberg*, July 19, 2019, https://www.bloomberg.com/news/articles/2019-07-19/divorce-destroys-finances-of-americans-over-50-studies-show#xj4y7vzkg; Angela A. Hung and David Knapp, "Impact of Divorce on Retirement Security," RAND, September 2017, https://www.rand.org/content/dam/rand/pubs/working_papers/WR1200/WR1201/RAND_WR1201.pdf.

8. Brian D'Onofrio and Robert Emery, "Parental Divorce or Separation and Children's Mental Health," *World Psychiatry* 18, no. 1 (February 2019), https://www.ncbi.nlm.nih.gov/pmc/articles/PMC6313686/.

9. Kerry Jamieson, "Aces and Divorce," Center for Child Counseling, February 25, 2019, https://www.centerforchildcounseling.org/aces-and-divorce/.

Chapter 2

1. See, for example, the 1984 Hair Club for Men commercial at https://www.youtube.com/watch?v=xeFoLdeqG1I.11.

Notes

2. Staff of the *Indiana Magazine of History*, "The Divorce Mill of the Midwest," Indiana Public Media, September 5, 2011, https://indianapublicmedia.org/momentofindianahistory/divorce-mill-midwest/.

Chapter 4

1. Oliver Tearle, "The Meaning and Origin of 'A Little Learning Is a Dangerous Thing,'" *Interesting Literature*, https://interestingliterature.com/2021/09/a-little-learning-is-a-dangerous-thing-meaning-analysis-origin/.

Chapter 5

1. American Sociological Association, "Women More Likely than Men to Initiate Divorces, but Not Non-marital Breakups," August 22, 2015, https://www.asanet.org/women-more-likely-men-initiate-divorces-not-non-marital-breakups/?hilite=divorce.

2. All statistics from Nathan Yau, "Divorce and Occupation," FlowingData, https://flowingdata.com/2017/07/25/divorce-and-occupation/.

3. Wilkinson and Finkbeiner, "Divorce Statistics: Over 115 Studies, Facts and Rates for 2022," accessed June 16, 2023, https://www.wf-lawyers.com/divorce-statistics-and-facts/.

4. Anneli Rufus, "Divorce Stats That Can Predict Your Marriage's Success," *Daily Beast*, July 14, 2017, https://www.thedailybeast.com/divorce-stats-that-can-predict-your-marriages-success/.

Chapter 6

1. All statistics from Wilkinson and Finkbeiner, "Divorce Statistics in the U.S. and Irvine, California," accessed June 16, 2023, https://www.orangecountydivorce.com/divorce-statistics-in-the-u-s-and-irvine-california/.

2. All statistics from Wilkinson and Finkbeiner, "Divorce Statistics in the U.S."

3. "Notwithstanding any other provision of this code, the court may base an award of attorney's fees and costs on the extent to which the conduct of each party or attorney furthers or frustrates the policy of the law to promote settlement of

litigation and, where possible, to reduce the cost of litigation by encouraging cooperation between the parties and attorneys. An award of attorney's fees and costs pursuant to this section is in the nature of a sanction. In making an award pursuant to this section, the court shall take into consideration all evidence concerning the parties' incomes, assets, and liabilities. The court shall not impose a sanction pursuant to this section that imposes an unreasonable financial burden on the party against whom the sanction is imposed. In order to obtain an award under this section, the party requesting an award of attorney's fees and costs is not required to demonstrate any financial need for the award."

Chapter 8

1. Christine Hammond, "Why Divorce Feels like a Death," *Psych Central*, November 2, 2018, https://psychcentral.com/pro/exhausted-woman/2018/11/why-divorce-feels-like-a-death#1.

2. Laura Broadwell, "Effects of Divorce on Children: An Age-by-Age Guide," *Parents*, July 28, 2022, https://www.parents.com/parenting/divorce/coping/age-by-age-guide-to-what-children-understand-about-divorce/.

3. Wayne Parker, "Should You Stay Together for the Kids?," *Verywell Family*, December 4, 2021, https://www.verywellfamily.com/should-you-stay-together-for-kids-1270800; David Schwartz, "Don't Stay Together for the Kids," *Psychology Today*, May 7, 2021, https://www.psychologytoday.com/us/blog/adolescents-explained/202105/don-t-stay-together-the-kids.

Chapter 9

1. Malcolm Gladwell, *Blink: The Power of Thinking without Thinking* (New York: Little, Brown, 2005).

2. Jerry Seinfeld, *Seinfeld*, season 4, episode 15, "The Visa," aired January 27, 1993, on NBC.

ABOUT THE AUTHORS

**Paul Nelson** is the founder of California firm Nelson Kirkman Family Law Attorneys. Certified by the State Bar of California Board of Legal Specialization in family law, he has extensive courtroom experience and knowledge of California family law, which have helped him build an impressive track record of successful outcomes for a wide range of clients. Paul is rated highly with Super Lawyers, possesses twenty five-star ratings with Avvo, and enjoys the highest ranking with Martindale-Hubbell.

Active in the legal community, Paul has published numerous articles in the *Orange County Business Journal*, *Forbes*, and *Fortune*. He is a member of the Orange County Bar Association, the State Bar of California, and the J. Reuben Clark Law Society. In his free time, Paul volunteers at the Veteran's Legal Institute, working tirelessly to address obstacles keeping our military veterans from the benefits they deserve.

Paul also serves on the board of the William Gray Inn of Court, whose core principle is to promote nationwide legal excellence and ethics. Specializing in complex, high-asset family law proceedings, Paul excels at producing the most favorable outcomes for his many clients, allowing them to get on with their lives—and their business.

Michael Ashley is a former Disney screenwriter and the author of more than thirty-five books on numerous subjects. He coauthored *Own the A.I. Revolution*, which launched at the United Nations and was named by Soundview as one of 2019's top business books.

A columnist for *Forbes* and *Becker's Hospital Review*, Michael serves as a member of City AI, an organization enabling the responsible development and application of artificial intelligence. An in-demand keynoter, he is also an official speaker for Vistage.

Michael taught screenwriting as a professor at Chapman University. His writing has been featured on KTLA and Fox Sports Radio and in *Entertainment Weekly*, *HuffPost*, *Newsbase*, *Fast Company*, the *National Examiner*, the United Nation's *ITU News Magazine*, the *Orange County Business Journal*, and the *Orange County Register*.

Made in the USA
Middletown, DE
30 January 2024